"If you are committed to 'growing your business' by selling more, invest the time to read this book and apply the concepts Alice introduces. Our sales team attended a training program based upon the book, but custom-designed by Alice, and within three weeks, I noticed a change in the activity and approach adopted by the team. Alice is able to relate to real-life sales issues and provided the team with solutions they could implement immediately. I achieved my ROI!"

ECKY PILZ, President, *Care Factor Computer Solutions, Inc.*

"This is an exciting book that will give you exactly what you need to excel in sales! Alice Wheaton's proven track record qualifies her to be your mentor. With the knowledge you will acquire, you can develop the confidence and competence to help your clients achieve their goals as you achieve yours. Alice has provided a very important service and innumerable people will benefit from it! *Say No to Me!* is a must-read!"

JUDY BUSH, Manager, Sales Education, The Americas, *Mary Kay, Inc.*

"What a surprise to find that the information in this book is not only applicable to my sales team but is applicable to all of the employees in the organization. Not only that, the information can be applied with great effectiveness to everyday life! Everyone, no matter what their title, is in sales and this book will help them get closer to success!"

TERRY O'GRADY, President & COO, *Stone Creek Properties, Inc.*

"*Say NO to Me!* shows you how to sell more, faster and easier, against any competition in any market. By removing objections skilfully, you move onto the high road to sales success."

BRIAN TRACY, author of
The 21 Success Secrets of Self-Made Millionaires, Eat that Frog!
and *The 100 Absolutely Unbreakable Laws of Business Success*

"As Alice Wheaton points out in her enlightening book, you ought to feel very good when a prospect says no to you. It's the first step towards that same prospect saying yes! Most people quit at that first no, but readers of *Say NO to Me!* will realize that it's really the halfway point in closing the sale. Congratulations to Alice for writing a book that salespeople around the world will hail as a breakthrough."

JAY CONRAD LEVINSON, author of the book series *Guerrilla Marketing*

"What an eye-opener! Anyone who still struggles with selling their goods or services because of the objections they hear NEEDS this book now. *Say NO to Me!* has to be the ultimate guide to overcoming objections, fears, and any self-sabotage. Get it!"

JOE VITALE, President, *Hypnotic Marketing, Inc.*
and best-selling author of *Spiritual Marketing*

"Alice Wheaton has written a book you can't refuse to read because her expertise is in how to overcome rejection, objection, and dejection. So stop trying to fight it, read the book and learn how to sell to anyone, at any time, from the master."

ALAN WEISS, PhD, author of *Million Dollar Consulting*

Say NO to Me!

The True Power of Upside-Down Selling

Alice Wheaton

© 2003 Alice Wheaton and CoreGrowth Foundations Inc.
2007 Second Impression

All rights reserved. No part of this publication may be reproduced, stored in a retrieval system, or transmitted in any form or by any means— electronic, mechanical, photocopying, recording, or otherwise—without the prior written permission of the copyright holder.

Published by CoreGrowth Foundations Inc.
Suite 1844, Westhills Town Center
Calgary, Alberta T3H 3C8
CANADA
www.alicewheaton.com
Toll Free: 1 (877) 542 • 5423

National Library of Canada Cataloguing in Publication Data

Wheaton, Alice, 1951–
    Say no to me! : The true power of upside-down selling/
Alice Wheaton.

    Includes index.
    ISBN: 0-9730366-2-1

    1. Selling. I. Title
HF5438.25.W358 2003   658.85   C2003–910325–0

CREDITS
Editing: Wayne Magnuson, *Prairie House Books*, Calgary, Alberta.
Proofreading: Robert Este, Canmore, Alberta.
Index: Elizabeth Bell, *Pinpoint Indexing*, Calgary, Alberta.
Cover, interior design & project management: Jeremy Drought,
Last Impression Publishing Service, Calgary, Alberta.

Printed and bound in CANADA by *Friesens*, Altona, Manitoba.

Dedication

THIS BOOK IS DEDICATED TO SOMEONE WHO WAS INSTRUMENTAL in facilitating my business success. Darrell Bennett, a good friend, has been a consistent source of encouragement, advice, and support. My wish for the world is that everyone with a dream should be so lucky as to have someone like Darrell in his or her corner!

How to Reach Us

To book ALICE WHEATON, for a keynote, half-day or full-day presentation, please contact her, toll free in North America, at **1(877) 542•5423**. To review other video, audio and text resources by Alice Wheaton, please visit her website. To order any resources, you may write, phone, fax, or e-mail Alice at:

CoreGrowth Foundations Inc.
Suite 1844, Westhills Town Center
Calgary, Alberta T3H 3C8
CANADA
Toll Free: 1 (877) 542•5423
Phone: (403) 249•5853
Fax: (403) 249•3514
E-mail: alice@alicewheaton.com

Acknowledgments

I WILL ALWAYS BE GRATEFUL TO CAL AND EDITH WENZEL, because the retainer with their company, *Shane Homes*, in my first year of self-employment created a foundation from which to grow my business. Working with them and their team at *Shane Homes* was such a pleasure. I will forever be grateful.

I thank my teenage son, Lloyd Worth, for his wit and excellent style of reflecting back to me the work that I do. He is a master of the art of negotiation and can deal with any objection I ever raise. My father, Newton Wheaton, was such a great parent that I still enjoy pleasing him. His pride in even the smallest of my successes fueled my courage to work towards the fulfillment of my greatest dreams. Whether I failed or succeeded, his comments were always the same: "It doesn't matter. You're my daughter and whatever you do fine by me."

My thanks are also extended to Lisbeth Corbier—her *Office and Home Maintenance Company* creates comfort for me when all else seems chaotic; Alden Snyder is someone I call on when my capacity to make things work is depleted; Clara Hornby brilliantly organizes me and all of the details around me and my gratitude for the peace of mind she brings me is immense; Harvey Sayles is truly a "computer whisperer" and the health of my computer is dependent on his interventions; Geoff Martin was a great support when my son was young and I needed to travel. Because of him, I never worried about my son or my pets whenever I was away from home.

My friends are the "strength behind my strength." You know who you are but I want to mention you anyway. Lorraine King, whom I always call first—whether I am in a quandary or when I have good news to share. I never tire of her spin on any issue. Aine Curran has been my friend for over twenty years. Even though we live at opposite ends of the country we've stayed in touch and, despite the distance, our connection grows stronger. Bev Chinnery challenges me with her practical advice and raw honesty. Cathy

Jamison is my resilient friend who radiates elegance and grace. Elaine Evans models sheer determination and discipline. I am grateful to Hazel Scott for her keen eye for grammar and sentence structure. She read this manuscript over and over again in its initial drafts. That is a sign of a true friend. Peggy Wall is a good friend with an eye for editorial detail. She made this manuscript part of her vacation reading material! Jim English also contributed to the editing of early drafts of the manuscript and he too has my sincere thanks.

Valerie McIlroy changed my life with one comment while I was still a nurse: "You would do well in sales. Why don't you interview at *Xerox*? I'll give you my husband's name to use as a reference." She did just that and it was the beginning of my love affair with the sales process, change management, and personal growth. With those few words, she set in motion life-altering events. I thank her from the bottom of my heart. Bill Irwin was the person who hired me at *Xerox* and taught me the skills to become a Big Game Hunter and Closer. He always encouraged me to show up bigger than I felt. Recently, I had the pleasure of speaking to Bill again and thanked him for his early mentorship.

A special thanks is extended to Peter Kuelker and Alain Audet of *Stonetile (Canada) Ltd.* Their sales team—Rob Dykstra, Joe Black, Tom Rayment, and Candice Beninger—has embraced the principles presented in this book. They confirm eight out of ten appointments from their cold calling efforts and have mastered the true power of Upside-down Selling! In fact, they have become so adept at dancing with objections and turning them into the juice of the sale that they express disappointment when no objections are forthcoming. They have become Alpha Sellers who revel in Big Game Hunting and Closing.

Finally, Casey and Clarence, my two cats, who like to sleep on top of whatever I write, lend support by encouraging me to take time out and focus on them!

Alice Wheaton, MA
Calgary, Alberta
October 2002

Table of Contents

Introduction
1

Chapter 1

Objections Are the Juice of the Sale!
15

Chapter 2

Internal Objections that Sabotage Success

29

Chapter 3

How to Manage Emotions & Feelings

43

Chapter 4

The Hazards of Perfectionism

49

Chapter 5

The Confidence Myth

55

Chapter 6

Questions Are the Answer, Aren't They?

61

Chapter 7

Needs Assessments Resolve Objections

71

Chapter 8

Problems are like Icebergs—Really!

77

Chapter 9

Price—The Mother of all Objections

89

Chapter 10

Warm Up the Cold Call

99

Chapter 11

Break Out of Voice Mail Jail

109

Chapter 12

Generic Sales Industry Objections

115

Chapter 13

Problem Situations that Threaten the Sale

123

Chapter 14
The Million Dollar Script
131

Conclusion
Mastering the Inner & Outer Objections
139

Appendix A
Network & Multi-level Marketing
143

Appendix B
The New Home Buyer
151

Glossary
163

Index
169

Foreword

by Alan Weiss, PhD

IN MY EXPERIENCE WORKING WITH ENTREPRENEURS ALL OVER THE WORLD, most advice about how to succeed misses the mark because it's based on conventional wisdom. Hence, people are advised to make certain they aren't undercapitalized, that they have a comprehensive business plan, and that they zealously safeguard their intellectual property.

Convention wisdom is exactly that: It's a mindlessly repeated mantra from people who haven't bothered to actually experience the contemporary environment. I believe that all entrepreneurs are primarily and fundamentally in the marketing business—despite the grandeur of their technology or the charisma of their personality—and the faster they become adept at marketing, the greater their success (which can be spectacularly rapid). Consequently, the greatest challenge facing these neophyte marketers is lack of self-esteem, particularly as it applies to convincing others that they have what those others need.

This is a book about the absolute hardest aspect of such marketing—cold calling and front-line selling. And it's a book meant for the beginner as well as veteran, because cold calling is not a skill that develops naturally. In fact, it's often antithetical to entrepreneurs' basic behaviors, and it's far more nuanced than the stereotypical "work the phones" and "just keep beating on the door."

Think about it: Have you ever bought investment services from the slick stranger who interrupts your life with a phone call at eight in the evening?

Alice Wheaton has thought about it and she's provided a rare glimpse into the workings of the true sales process. It's about work, it's about discipline, and it's inevitably linked to rejection. But it's not impossible. In fact, it's as essential aspect of every successful entrepreneur's highlight film.

Selling is about the true belief that you are providing value for someone who needs it and is able to purchase it. This book will help you recognize your value proposition, identify the buyer, work around "gate-keepers," and provide a compelling set of reasons for your prospect to, first, speak to you and, second, agree to become a client or customer.

There is a plethora of books on the shelves about selling, and that's because the topic is critical and the need vast, but also because no one source has provided the comprehensive range of techniques and methodology for every situation and every personality. That makes sense.

This book is an important addition to the genre because it provides the process for selling, literally, to strangers and for reaching those often thought to be unreachable. We can never avoid rejection, but we can certainly reduce both its frequency and its consequences, personally as well as professionally. To be successful, all of us must continually attract new business, which means new buyers, which means people who have no idea about who we are or how we can help.

It's our responsibility to improve their lot, and Alice has taken on the responsibility of helping you to do just that.

Alan Weiss, PhD
President, *Summit Consulting Group, Inc.*
Author, *Million Dollar Consulting*
and *The Ultimate Consultant Library*
East Greenwich, Rhode Island
February, 2003

Introduction

O VER TEN YEARS OF WORKING WITH THOUSANDS OF SALES PEOPLE and hundreds of sales teams, I have learned to begin each training session by asking: *What specific objections do you receive when you are either prospecting on the phone or when you are selling your product or service?*

Without fail, this question has always been met with a considerable number of blank stares. The fact is that most sales people do not know what their sales objections are. A review of the literature related to sales training reveals many general discussions of objections, but I have yet to find an adequate treatment of the subject of handling sales objections.

One of the reasons I was always among the top sales personnel—in several sales positions with different organizations—was my willingness to uncover as many and perhaps all of my clients' objections. As I uncovered one objection after another, I was able to be proactive, and deal with the concerns of my customers. The early lesson was: *Objections are the juice of the sale.* Not only did I want to understand why my product worked for my client, I also wanted to understand why it might not work. I sought the complete picture, which always contains negative, as well as positive, information.

When a salesperson is unafraid of their client's concerns, limitations, or lack of knowledge, they are able to delve into the whole story and, more often than not, clear up misinformation the client would have otherwise failed to disclose. This approach is totally *upside-down*, or opposite, from what other experts recommend. Salespeople, then and now, were and are encouraged to ask their customers patronizing questions designed to elicit a series of *yes* answers. Many salespeople are afraid to hear *no* and use a great deal of energy avoiding this reaction. They would rather receive an insincere *yes* than work with the *no*. I refer to this as *Happy Ears Syndrome.* Those who suffer from this syndrome would rather hear an insincere *yes*, and be duped out of a sale, than receive

1

and handle an objection—through discussion and problem-solving—which could lead to a sale. The unwillingness to be comfortable with a client's concerns is one of the main reasons why so many salespeople quit after the first call. If ignoring objections really worked, far more salespeople would be successful.

In general, why is it that sales people do not actively search for problems, invite clients to express their concerns and embrace the objections? I believe there are three major reasons that prevent this vigilance.

The first reason is that all of us have been told—repeatedly—to be "positive thinkers." At work, our supervisor or manager expresses concern if we present ourselves as anything less than upbeat, positive, self-assured, and in control. Doubt was not encouraged, so we moved into a state of passivity and denial-in a way, training ourselves to avoid reality.

The second reason is that sales people feel powerless when they receive objections because they haven't learned how to respond to them with elegance and grace. Typically, when a salesperson receives an objection, he or she feels disagreed with which then leads to them feeling disapproved of, which of course leads to feeling rejected and becoming internally dismantled. They just have not learned to positively engage with the customer through the objection. They do not know how to actually embrace the objection and then use it to forward a greater understanding of the unique needs of the client. Salespeople do not know that a prospect who does not present an objection will be unlikely to become a client. An objection is a point of engagement.

The third reason is that we have been taught to handle objections in a combative manner. In so doing we show our clients just how stupid they are to have the concern. For instance, we have been trained to respond to a pricing objection by saying: *How much too expensive is it?* or: *If I can get it for you for $X less, will you want to take delivery?* These responses do not give us any indication of the issues, needs, or concerns behind the objection.

The solution to *fear of rejection* is opening yourself up to the possibility of being rejected and accepting it as just a *no* and not a personal affront. It's important to change the idea that you must be well received and reach agreement in every interaction you engage in. Life is just not like that. The willingness to accept and welcome a *no* is one of the most important factors in your success. This 'simple' shift in mindset will allow you to show up *bigger* than you feel and achieve much more than you thought you could. Becoming detached from receiving either a *yes* or a *no* will help keep you calm, and allow you to become a true professional. Giving your customers and prospects permission to say *no* in this manner is *upside-down* from many traditionally recommended selling strategies.

Another trait common to salespeople is their tendency to talk 'features and benefits.' The *Upside-down strategy* is to go beyond benefits into *value*. Traditionally, when a client presents a problem, the salesperson immediately offers a solution. *The Upside-down strategy* is forget your solution for the moment and encourage the client to tell you much more about the problem and the inconveniences this problem causes. Not to be outdone, when a client makes a statement, the traditional salesperson steals the show, as it were, and segues into 'the pitch.' The *Upside-down strategy*, however, is to keep quiet and encourage the client to disclose yet further details. This dispels the myth that to be a good salesperson one must necessarily be a smooth talker. Instead, one must always attend to the client with concerned inquiry. Another *Upside-down strategy* is to never answer a question unless you know the source and context of that question.

In reading this book, you will learn how to edge out your competition by conducting a needs/issues assessment and thereby have an effective process for discovering your customer's concerns, questions, conditions, and objections. This will be completed elegantly without the need to ask rhetorical questions that pin your customer to the wall.

Let me tell you a story that exemplifies the value of handing objections rather than being overwhelmed by them yourself.

Recently I had the pleasure of meeting my friend's mother for the first time. She is a most elegant, poised, and beautiful eighty year old woman. With twinkling eyes, she told me about a day when John was only eight years old and he came home crying because the bully next door had frightened him and attempted to hit him with a stick. His mom told me she didn't like having a son who wouldn't defend himself. So, she promised him that if he took the stick away from the bully she'd pay him sixpence (this happened in England) at which point John became even more upset! He wanted to defeat the bully and earn the money but couldn't see how he could ever accomplish this.

His mom then gave him a remarkable demonstration. She handed him a broom, and directed him to hit her with it. As he tried to hit her, she stepped in so close to him that he couldn't swing the broom. She grabbed the broom and took it away from him. They practiced this technique over and over again, right there in her kitchen. Finally John was willing, though he was not sure if he was ready, to confront his tormenter. He ventured outside in search of the bully. He admits now that it was the lure of sixpence as well as the need for justice that had spurred him on. Nevertheless, can you imagine how fearful he was? Finally, the bully appeared and, sure enough he got in close and easily wrenched the stick away from his tormentor. It was the bully's turn then to run home crying.

The lesson he learned was *the stick was a more effective weapon for the bully only if he had room to swing it. By daring to close the distance, and get in close to the threatening stick, he had eliminated its power and effectiveness.*

The lesson of the swinging stick is a metaphor for handling sales objections. Those sales people who are afraid of objections stand back, giving the objections maximum power over their sales effectiveness. However, the sales person who is willing and able to step in close and learn all about the objection is the one who eliminates the objection as a threat and will use the objection to advance the sale.

It is a natural human tendency to avoid conflict, but discovering and resolving objections can occur in an elegant manner while showing respect for both ourselves and our clients. In order to have success and contentment in the future, one must be willing to deal with the discomfort and pain of the moment. Providing guidelines and suggestions for how to do this successfully and with grace is the purpose of this book.

One of the attitudes I want to shatter is the idea that there is no point in trying to overcome objections because there are too many objections to overcome. My research reveals that you are likely to receive no more than six objections when prospecting by phone, and there are only a further six objections specific to your sector of the sales industry. That's a potential total of twelve objections-all of which are simple to learn and overcome.

In handling an objection, you need to know not only *what* to say, but *how* to say it. This is where you combine the principles of my *million dollar sales script* with your own personality. As no actor would go on stage without having studied a script, so you should not attempt to answer an objection without your script. Once on stage, the actor may add some personal style to the intonations, pace, and delivery. You can do the same with the scripts I provide.

To those sales people who claim to be opposed to the use of sales scripts, I offer the following challenge: let me observe you during three client appointments, and I guarantee that I will be able to predict your script and pattern for the fourth call. Since you already use a sales script, let's make it one that works *by design instead of happenstance.*

There are probably six frequently encountered objections specific to your sector of the sales industry, but these are also remarkably generic. A commercial banker and a software developer will both have heard a version of: *I dealt with you before, and I wasn't happy, Your product/service costs too much, I already have a supplier I'm happy with, I'm not interested at this time, Your turnaround time is too long,* and *We have no need of your product/service.* I offer some common sense responses to these common industry objections from which salespeople from a wide spectrum of sales sectors will be able to extrapolate-and construct their own responses. You may also e-mail me directly with any other objections or situations not mentioned in this book, and I will post answers on my website. E-mail: **alice@alicewheaton.com**.

You may not be completely *confident* the first time you confront your customer's objections, just as John was not confident about confronting the bully after one stick-handling practice. But, like him, after several practice trials you will be *competent.* Once you feel competent, your longing for confidence will ease—I promise you. You will know first-hand that competence always comes before confidence.

Organization of this Book

I have organized this book to discuss and develop practical strategies for dealing with fear of confrontation and conflict in sales and marketing. Each of the book's fourteen chapters are filled with practical suggestions, processes and guidelines that have been tested, improved and successfully used to resolve psychological sales and marketing barriers. The book also features two very useful, value-added appendices. Appendix "A" addresses Network Marketing while Appendix "B" explores the situation of The New Home Buyer. These appendices are followed by a very useful glossary of terms that can be applied in any sales or marketing situation.

The layout of the fourteen chapters follows a clear and logical plan that guides you to explore and develop new and very practical sales strategies. Chapter one provides a simple process for locating hidden landmines and rendering them harmless. This is done in a straightforward and respectful manner, both towards the salesperson and the client. With this process you edge out the competition, build trust, and sell value. The result is that the mother of all objections—price—becomes the least important objection of all.

In Chapter Two I discuss the most difficult personal, internal objections that may not be so easily accessible to your own psyche or thinking because they are buried in your subconscious. It seems that one of the operating rules of our ego is to keep us small and manageable; however, once we know our own limitations and weaknesses, we do something about what we have discovered—we grow. To access this growth, please be your own devil's advocate when you read about internal objections, and declare: *Yes, I have that. Now, what am I going to do to diminish it?* Become a "one-percenter" by showing up to do the best you can for the day. You will find that even a one percent improvement will be met with positive results. Very soon you will be able to shift your thoughts from: *I'm doing the best I can for today, to: My best just got better!*

Managing emotions and feelings is vital to success. Chapter Three outlines specific and effective processes for developing this necessary skill set. Perfectionism is an impossible goal of this management, however, and Chapter Four provides you with an alternative model for successfully developing skills and personal mastery.

Courage, not confidence, is the answer to peak performance. Chapter Five outlines the path from fear to courage, from courage to competence and from competence to confidence. Chapter Six then details how to practice concerned inquiry and discover your customers' needs. Those needs or issues can be tracked by conducting a formal Needs/Issues Assessment as prescribed in Chapter Seven.

Problems and icebergs have much in common. It is not the obvious issues that motivate clients to buy, but the hidden issues. You will learn how to uncover these issues in Chapter Eight.

I have given price its own chapter because it is such an obstacle both for salespeople and their clients. You must learn to undo what our mass marketing has done, which is to train our customers to think almost exclusively of price. "We won't be undersold" and "Lowest prices in town" are just two of the messages we always see and hear, and eventually we begin to think of every purchase only in terms of a price purchase. Most salespeople don't know how to dismantle these thought processes for themselves, let alone their prospects. Speaking the "language of value" as well as the language necessary for the price or cost buyer is one of the pieces to the puzzling process of selling value. In Chapter Nine you will learn the language of all three levels of buyer: price, cost and value.

Chapter Ten shows you how to warm up your next cold call by providing responses to the six most common objections received when making such calls by telephone—the way most cold calls are made, as opposed to showing up in person. These six objections can strike terror into the hearts of salespeople when prospecting and cold calling. They know that when they make the call they will receive objections, and unless they can address those objections appropriately, they will feel intimidated and even stupid (note that this topic is discussed in greater detail in another book I have written entitled: *Prospect and Prosper: Cold Calling Strategies for the Feint of Heart*).

Voice Mail Jail is the bane of every salesperson's existence. Chapter Eleven provides strategies that will ease this torment. Even if your message is never returned, you must leave a lasting impression. Mundane messages do not stand out from the crowd.

Chapters Twelve and Thirteen contain general case-based examples of objections and situations that threaten sales. While the examples may not fit your specific sector in the sales industry, you will still benefit from reading these examples because you should be able to identify predictable patterns and solutions that you can apply to your particular sector and the objections or situations you do experience.

Try not to become too frustrated as you read others' objections. Use the examples to think about and create your own processes and, if you ever get stuck and want a specific answer, remember you can always e-mail me at: **alice@alicewheaton.com**.

The central text of the book finishes with Chapter Fourteen. This chapter provides a million dollar script that you can use as a template for shaping success with your unique objections. The script has this name because if you create your own script abiding by the principles provided and incorporate them within your personality, you will sell millions of dollars worth of products and services!

The two appendices which address network marketing and the new home buyer then round off the suggestions and guidelines provided throughout the main text. Appendix "A" on network marketing is based on my own experience in the health-care industry but can be applied to any business sector. Network marketing is most appealing to the emerging entrepreneur who is contemplating building a first-rate sales team. This appendix addresses network marketing objections and recruitment approaches.

I have devoted appendix "B" to the new home buyer because a new home is, for most people, the most expensive purchase anyone will ever make in their entire lifetime! Every parade of new show homes is usually comprised of several home builders, each working hard to downplay the degree to which they are competing with each other for the new home buyer's business. All of them anticipate that clients will bring their design ideas with them and shop one builder against the other. The new home salesperson who follows the processes outlined in appendix "B" (and indeed, throughout this entire book) will gain customer loyalty and sell more homes.

Creating new responses to sales objections—and dancing with them rather than avoiding them—will increase your success and help you break through into the big leagues. You will be able to join the ranks of the *super sellers* who command a signing bonus just for joining the company!

This book provides you with the examples, openings and opportunities to learn how to do all of these things and do them well. By reading this book, and then thinking about and applying what you learn, you can begin to build the foundation for your future success—now.

If not now, when?

A Story About My Beginning

You may be wondering about my own foundation for what this book is about. How did I come to know these things? What about my own experience? What follows is a brief account of how I started my career in sales. I had no specific skills for acquiring and developing new clients. I also knew very little about cold calling, prospecting or handling objections. But I learned and succeeded, and now I am relating what I know so that you can succeed, too. Let my beginning be an inspiration to all—every one of these skills can be *learned*, and *learned well*.

In 1978 I joined *Xerox Canada* as the first woman photocopier sales representative on the team. The interview process was long and arduous. There were several "strikes" against me, or objections presented as to why I couldn't be hired. The first objection was openly discussed with me...I was a woman. The second objection was that I was a nurse, "not a salesperson," and so how could an ex-intensive care nurse cope with the change in careers? The third and biggest objection: *You have no sales experience and there are several men, each with an MBA and sales experience applying for the position.* Although these objections seem archaic now, they were real at the time.

How I got to *Xerox* in the first place is a story in and of itself. It all started with a beautiful woman—Valerie McIlroy! Having been involved in a minor accident, she was admitted to the emergency room of a local hospital where I happened to be a nurse. Given the context, the contrast in our respective physical appearances was startling. She was dressed beautifully—as she had been on her way to a party—whereas I was "stuck" on the evening shift, wearing a shapeless uniform. Her purse and shoes matched, the clothes she wore were obviously expensive, and she looked glamorous!

I asked Valerie what she did for a living and she told me she was in advertising sales for *Yellow Pages*. Instantly—out of my mouth—came the words: *That's what I want to do. Whom would I talk to at your company to get a job doing what you do?* While she encouraged me to consider a career in sales, I was advised not to talk to her company unless I had some experience interviewing for similar positions. She suggested I approach Xerox instead and use her husband's name. *They aren't hiring women there yet, but they'll give you an interview and you will learn some great skills in the process which will help you in interviewing for other sales positions.*

The very next day, I dropped by *Xerox*, filled out an application form and left it at the front desk. My next step was to go shopping. I bought several suits and a briefcase in preparation for the interviews I felt sure would occur. I left the store with a wardrobe appropriate to a woman in business and my image of myself began to change. This was the first step in reinventing myself—effecting a transformation from nurse to salesperson.

What I remember most clearly from my first meeting with *Xerox* was the answer I gave when asked why I thought myself qualified for the job. I replied: *I'm not shy.* The interviewer commented that my negative approach to a positive character trait bothered him and he asked me to rephrase my statement in a positive manner. I said: *Fine then, I'm positive that I'm not shy.* He began to laugh and I was sent to my first of seven interviews with various sales managers and the branch manager. I learned two lessons during the interviewing process. One was the role of humor and that being able to laugh at oneself is vital in any situation. The second lesson was to not take anything personally, otherwise I would never have been able to keep an upbeat attitude during what proved to be an arduous process. My first interview was with Bill Irwin—the *Silver Fox*, as his sales team called him. It was devotion at first sight for me. My gut instinct was so strong about him that I very quickly decided I wanted to work for *Xerox* and, given the choice, I wanted Bill to be my manager.

After the sixth interview and multiple psychological tests, Bill agreed I had a strong aptitude for sales. He said he was beginning to *consider* hiring me but was vacillating over the decision because he had no experience in managing women. Bill managed the most successful sales team in that branch office, and he didn't want to risk introducing another variable that might have less than positive ramifications. Although I knew about his concerns, I continued to ask Bill for the job each time I spoke to him. Finally, in exasperation, he admitted that his beliefs were changing but to be sure he'd have to interview my husband to confirm whether I could have the job (you should recall that this was 1978 and, by this point, I wanted the job so badly I would have bought Bill a plane ticket to interview my parents—if it would have helped him decide).

Bill met with my husband who simply stated that my career choices were up to me. As he left our home, Bill told me he would call me the next day to let me know his final decision. That day, Friday, came and went with no call, so I told myself he'd call on Saturday or Sunday. But, he never did call. On Monday, I got up, got dressed in one of my new business suits, took an empty briefcase and set out for the *Xerox* office.

I went in an hour before anyone else and sat quietly and fearfully at one of the salesmen's desks. When Bill arrived, he was visibly surprised, and asked what I was doing there. I replied: *Well, I missed your call. No news is good news so if you show me how to pack my briefcase I'll go to work for you today.* With a displeased look, Bill ushered me into his office where he told me he was still undecided. So, once more, I began the closing process. This time I was specific, and used the "Ben Franklin Close" which was on one of the sales tapes by J. Douglas Edwards I had listened to over and over again. It goes something like this.

"Mr. Irwin, wouldn't you agree that Ben Franklin was one of the world's wisest men, and when he was faced with a difficult choice he wanted to make the best decision. Isn't that what you want to do in hiring or not hiring me—make the right decision? So here's what he would do. He'd take a piece of paper and draw a line down the middle and on the right side he'd list all of the reasons not to hire me and on the left he'd write all of the reasons to hire me. Can we do that one thing before I go and then I promise not to ask you for the job again? Does this sound fair to you?"

Bill agreed that this was fair so I began listing all of the reasons to hire me. When I had helped him identify at least eight good reasons it was time to list the negative reasons. I did what the tape suggested and shut up. I folded my hands and looked at him and smiled. He had received my help and was now conditioned to depend on my negative suggestions. Except, none were forthcoming.

When I'd finished my closing process, Bill laughed and asked me where I'd learned it. I confessed that I had been preparing myself by listening to tapes by J. Douglas Edwards on selling and closing. He was amazed. He told me he had taken his sales team to hear Mr. Douglas speak at a seminar and that he had bought each one of his salesmen a complete set of tapes. *The Ben Franklin Close*, as this particular close was called, was the very same technique he had requested his sales team memorize and then role-play at sales meetings and yet each member of his team had resisted.

Bill offered me the job and it was only then that I realized that success comes from being willing to do whatever others don't want to do.

One condition of my appointment was that I was asked to promise never to cry if I was criticized in a sales training session. I showed my confusion over such a strange request and learned that apparently this had nothing to do with my being a woman. It was because most of the men before me had cried and Bill knew how to deal with a male trainee crying but not with a female trainee crying.

Thus began my sales career. I vacillated between feeling lucky and feeling frightened and anxious. I discovered that if I put my ego aside and did exactly as I was told by my manager, I would achieve the promised results. So I kept doing what worked and the next year I achieved an amazing 198% of plan—almost double my target sales goal.

Adjusting to the sales system had its challenges, including my integration with the sales team. I learned to have two sales deals in my briefcase for the end of each month. One of those deals was to post on the team order board on the last business day of the month. I would make sure I was the last to leave the office after having posted the order-even if it meant my staying until midnight to achieve it! The second deal was for the next business day, the beginning of the new month. In this way, I figured I could "bracket" all the sales of other reps and keep my name appearing frequently on the team order board. In hindsight, I see this ploy as partly a function of my competitive spirit but it was also my way of managing my fear, doubts and insecurities, and wanting to feel better about myself.

While I told no one of this strategy, Bill must have figured it out quite easily. Whenever there was a Sales Manager's contest, he'd ask me if I were "sandbagging," which means holding deals back instead of entering them into the sales system. During contests, I'd relent and do what I had to in order to replace the orders I was saving. I never held back on logging orders he needed for a Sales Manager's contest because I held him in such high esteem—and still do. He was my mentor and my hero. Every new salesperson entering the industry then or now would have been well served by a manager like him. Almost twenty years later, I find myself mentoring, encouraging and working with others, just as Bill did for and with me.

Each of us can leave a lasting, tangible effect on another person and thus, by extension, the world. One way to accomplish this is through the spoken word, just as that patient I met in the emergency room did for me—by encouraging me to go to *Xerox* for my first interview. A second is through the written word. That is the purpose of this book—so you can learn about what worked for me. As Ben Franklin also said: *The wise learn from their own mistakes but the intelligent learn from someone else's.*

Integrate the techniques I describe in this book with your own personality and style, apply them in your business and professional activities, and you will experience a greater level of success in your life—I promise!

Chapter 1

Objections Are the Juice of the Sale!

ALESPEOPLE GENERALLY DON'T KNOW THIS, but there are two main reasons why prospects raise objections. First, objections work to get rid of incompetent salespeople, and second, they help separate good salespeople from the rest of the pack who do not know objections are worth their weight in gold—and are the juice of the sale!

Each time you receive, acknowledge and deal with an objection during the prospecting call, your chances of getting the appointment will increase by about 25%. If you were to ask for an appointment three times and you successfully dealt with any and all objections on each occasion, you would have raised your chances of getting an appointment to 75%. Occasionally, a prospect will become annoyed with this sort of persistence. Do not let the reaction of five percent of your contacts influence the way you approach the other 95%.

Not backing down demonstrates a belief in yourself and in your product or service. You are seen as a leader, a person who respects the burning desire to succeed. Those who can manage their uncomfortable emotions well enough, who ask again and again for a desired outcome, demonstrate personal power. Some readers may be asking: *Won't clients get angry if I continue to ask them for an appointment?* The answer to this question is going to vary with every potential client. If you carefully integrate the request for a meeting with a clear respect for client concerns, you are not likely to cause offence.

People with power are comforted by displays of power. If you are seen as being reticent, your "power clients" will presume you're likely to waste their time. They have their own power so they don't need anyone

> *Those who can manage their uncomfortable emotions well enough, who ask again and again for a desired outcome, demonstrate personal power.*

to be submissive to them. If you are unable to handle a few objections, you will be relegated to the role of a lower-level decision maker, which is where you belong. This may sound harsh, but it is true. You must see yourself as the equal—a peer—of your clients. You have something of value to offer them and they have a problem that you can solve for them. It's an ideal match!

> You must see yourself as the equal—a peer—of your clients. You have something of value to offer them and they have a problem that you can solve for them. It's an ideal match!

Salespeople must expect to receive objections from prospects. Those who do not accept this will fall by the wayside. Prospects present objections because they know objections intimidate salespeople and keep them away. In his book, *Can I Have Five Minutes of Your Time?* Hal Becker states that 50% of salespeople quit after the first call. As far as the customer is concerned, objections work.

Analysis Paralysis

Faced with objections such as: *I already have a supplier I'm happy with*, most salespeople respond with: *Okay, thank you*. The salesperson feels disgruntled and rejected as he hangs up and, before making the next cold call, *Analysis Paralysis* can set in.

Analysis Paralysis stems from a mindset in which the victim focuses on the worst possible scenario. The mind becomes paralyzed with worry about what could go wrong. Fear becomes so strong that the salesperson may be unable to take the next step—phoning another client—because of the perils that lie ahead. For those suffering from *Analysis Paralysis*, fear of rejection is a real and significant roadblock on the selling trail. Many victims stop making cold calls altogether.

Fear of Rejection

There is no such thing as fear of rejection. There is, however, a fear that we will not be able to manage our emotions after we have been rejected. The moment when a client says *no* or gives another response that causes discomfort is just that—a moment in time. The story we tell ourselves about that moment is the cause of our trauma. We fail to recognize the truth: that an objection is not a personal rejection. An objection may be a rejection of our product or service; it is not a rejection of us.

Here's an example of misplaced fear of rejection. Imagine you are at a social event and you see someone you'd like to meet. You want to go over and ask him/her for a dance, but your negative self says: *Are you crazy? You go over there and you'll get a big fat NO, and on the way back to the table, everyone will be looking at you. They'll be thinking what a loser you are, they'll nudge each other and snicker and you'll feel foolish.* You've projected these thoughts into the future and accepted them as truth. You've imagined the worst possible scenario and convinced yourself that no other outcome is likely.

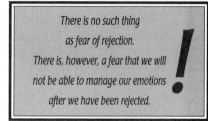

There is no such thing as fear of rejection. There is, however, a fear that we will not be able to manage our emotions after we have been rejected.

It is possible to undermine our future achievement by imposing a conditioned memory of how we felt the last time we were unsuccessful in achieving a desired outcome. The event we perceived as a rejection, compounded by our hurt feelings, has been intensified and blown out of proportion. Fearing we can't manage any more feelings of rejection, we have a tendency to shut down. The word FEAR is an acronym for *False Evidence Appearing Real.*

When the salesperson allows unhappy memories to impede progress, fear of rejection will create a self-fulfilling prophecy. When you confront a challenge, it's much easier to see yourself as a victim of rejection than it is to manage uncomfortable feelings. You decide you can't possibly handle rejection again so you don't even make the attempt. Imagine how much you're missing when you think and act in this manner.

Be Willing to Receive a *NO!*

The solution to fear of rejection is opening yourself up to the possibility of being rejected and accepting it as just a *no* and not a personal affront. It's important to change the idea that you must be well-received and reach agreement in every interaction you have. Life is just not like that. The willingness to accept and welcome a *no* is one of the most important factors in your success. This simple shift in mindset will allow you to show up *bigger* than you feel and achieve much more than you thought you could. Becoming detached from the words *yes* and *no* will help keep you calm and allow you to become a true professional.

There is a way to enroll the power of fear of rejection and that is to permit the client to say *no* to either you or your offer. This is reverse psychology, and it works. When I make a prospecting call or present a proposal to a prospect, I want the appointment or the opportunity with all my heart. Nevertheless, I am willing to be rejected. I have enough experience with rejection to know that it may sting a bit, but I will be safe. I will not implode, explode or in any other way come apart. My mind may have doubts, but I can choose to ignore them. However, it does help to ask for what you want in a way that will minimize your uncomfortable feelings if your request is rejected. One technique is to give people the right to say *no*, to court the possibility of rejection. In a business or social setting, we can ask in a way that gives both parties more comfort room: *I'd like to ask you to dance, but please feel free to say no if you don't want to.*

Giving customers or prospects the choice to say *no* in this manner is *upside down*—the very antithesis of most traditional theories of sales techniques. Typically, sales scripts and presentations have been developed to corner the client into agreeing with the salesperson. If this really worked there would be many *more super sellers*!

> ...giving people the option to say no makes it easier for them to say yes because it is human nature to respond well.
>
> People feel respected when given a choice over their actions, no matter how small that choice may appear to be.
>
> When we give people a choice, it creates receptivity by lowering their defenses.

In an office setting, we could say: *Mark, I need someone to help me move boxes from my office to the storage room, but please say no if it's not convenient.* When you give people the opportunity to say *no*, it reduces the pangs you feel associated with receiving a *no*, which is what most people call rejection. As you are expressing this option, you can be mentally preparing yourself for the possibility of receiving a *no*. Paradoxically, giving people the option to say *no* makes it easier for them to say *yes* because it is human nature to respond well. People feel respected when given a choice over their actions, no matter how small that choice may appear to be. When we give people a choice, it creates receptivity by lowering their defenses. Giving others a choice is the bedrock of respect. When they sense your respect, they become naturally receptive. *Yes* is much more likely to be their final answer!

Increase Respect with Choice

Asking for what you want from your clients, such as closing for the order or asking for an appointment, is no different—from a feelings point of view—than asking someone to dance. In both cases there is often a feeling of dread. This feeling is reduced when you give them permission, either verbally or in your own mindset, to say *no* to you.

The *no* often comes disguised as an objection or a complaint: it is therefore vital that you have sensitive ears. When you receive a *no* from the client, do not dismiss it; instead, embrace it. You need to know that clients and prospects say *no* in a variety of ways, some blatant and some subtle. Just as it is uncomfortable to receive a *no* when you ask for something, it is also hard for clients to say *no* (which is why we gave the person at the dance the choice). Some clients become creative in letting you down and still saving face. The *no* often comes disguised as a red herring in the form of an objection or critical statement.

One example of a clear *no* is the typical objection when calling for an appointment. The prospect might say: *I already have a supplier I am happy with*, or *I don't have time*. The typical salesperson would say: *Oh, okay. May I send you some printed material?* The client agrees and the salesperson is mollified. They now feel better. Their *Happy Ears Syndrome* has been abated once more because the prospect said yes to something.

> ...*customers have every right to say no, in whatever manner they choose, and you have every right to ask for what you want, again and again.*

It is vital to recognize—in every fiber of your being—that customers have every right to say *no*, in whatever manner they choose, and you have every right to ask for what you want, again and again.

In this cold-calling scenario, you could use the *upside-down* approach by responding: *Steve, this software package I represent is revolutionary.*

Question it, doubt it, clarify it, but please—don't miss out on discovering what it can do for your accounting process. If you agree to meet with me for an hour, I promise there will be no high-pressure selling. In fact, if you want to proceed, it will be at your invitation.

At the end of the appointment, there is nothing to stop you from saying: *Steve, I promised there would be no high-pressure selling. What do you think we should do? The choice is yours.* Once a question is asked, be quiet and let him answer. To speak before he answers is to go into high-pressure selling. If the answer is *no* to proceeding with the sales process or to further contact, respect that.

Another customer may use a subtle form of saying *no*. Let's say you are in a third meeting with Mary and it appears that you are a match. You decide to ask for her business. You reiterate what you believe her needs to be and then you pop the question: *Mary, do you see any reason why we can't be your supplier of choice?*

When Mary replies: *I hear you've been having difficulty with delivery,* do not become dismantled. Instead, be willing to explore the concern. You can present yourself as confident by being willing to delve into and explore any contentious issues. Stop talking and give Mary an opportunity to register and explore the issue with you in a non-confrontational manner.

It is vital to see any concern as a possible *no,* and know that this concern will become a block to future business if you dismiss it as unimportant. Encourage your customer to reveal and discuss all concerns. What is curious (and *upside-down*) is that after discussing concerns, clients and prospects often dismiss them. If they are not encouraged to explore their concerns and objections, they will continue to sit there—and block your business.

When you have an open and receptive attitude to whatever form of *no* the client raises, your business will grow. Your open, receptive attitude to receiving a *no* as well as a *yes* is perceived as respectful behavior on your part.

How to Discuss Objections/Concerns

You begin discussing client concerns by offering them the opportunity to do so. In typical sales scenarios, salespeople try to avoid confrontation by talking too much, too fast. If the client doesn't express disagreement with them, the company they represent or the product/service they sell, salespeople feel all is well and it has been a good sales call.

The process of *Upside-down selling* establishes that nothing could be further from the truth. You must be willing to entertain disagreement, dissension and especially dialogue, about contentious issues with your prospect.

Unfortunately, most people go into a downward spiral when they receive other than positive feedback. Someone disagrees with them and immediately they feel disapproval. Then they become dismantled inside and respond by either defending and justifying, or retreating from the process. This immature communication cycle actually holds in tyranny those with whom we have a relationship because it presumes they must express to us only that which we want to hear.

We Experience Disagreement
⬇
Feel Disapproved of
⬇
Become Dismantled Inside
⬇
React Defensively or Retreat

It bares repeating that many salespeople suffer from *Happy Ears Syndrome*. These people avoid objections at all costs, thereby missing out on forming mutually beneficial long-term business relationships.

Giving prospects and clients the option to say *no*, as demonstrated by being willing to receive their objection in an open manner, has four major benefits:

1. It creates receptivity by helping clients/prospects feel respected and not pushed into a corner.

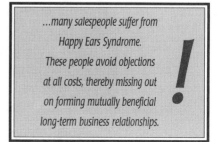

...many salespeople suffer from Happy Ears Syndrome. These people avoid objections at all costs, thereby missing out on forming mutually beneficial long-term business relationships.

2. You will project the impression of being someone who is confident, non-defensive and open to feedback of all kinds.

3. In eliciting more information from your clients—and thereby better understanding their needs—you will outmaneuver your competition and sell more. Would you want to deal with a salesperson who fails to understand the negative issues clients face in their work environment?

4. You will be regarded as more approachable because a person with fewer defenses and no discernible pretenses is much more likable.

Stickhandle Around the Objection

In the game of hockey, *stickhandling* refers to skillfully maneuvering the puck around opposing team members. In sales, client objections are the puck—you work with one at a time.

It's beneficial to recognize that an objection from a prospect is not a firm and final *no*. It is more like a *kNOw*. When objecting, a prospect wants to know more, or s/he wants to know that you can manage a few objections. This becomes an opportunity for you to know more by asking questions about specific concerns. You can reduce your knowledge gap by making use of the *Five kNOws*.

Close Early, Close Often

Ask yourself this question: *When do children stop asking for what they want? The answer: When they get it. So what makes children so much more tenacious and successful than adults?*

Children want what they want wholeheartedly and are willing to spend all their time and energy in the pursuit of whatever makes them happy. As children grow into contributing members of society, however, they are socialized to believe that it is inappropriate to pursue their wants with youthful passion. If we could recapture our youth, we could recapture the wonders that accompany getting what we want.

The Five kNOws to Know

1. Know how their overall business will be affected by your product or service.

2. Know what their needs are now, and project those needs for 1–5 years. Also, know what would stall the sales process. For example, what is their budget? What is their competitive position in the marketplace?

3. Know why they would choose you over your competitors.

4. Know where the product/service will be used and who else in the company might use it.

5. Know when to close. During each appointment, ask for the order or for a decision that moves you toward closing the sale. Close early and close often. One VP of sales recently complained: *I don't need relationship builders; I need closers!*

As adults, we need to remember that getting what we want isn't a matter of greediness or self-centered behavior. If you have a vision or a dream, you are not being self-centered if you want to make it come true. When a salesperson can integrate an adult level of understanding with the tenacity of a child, tremendous results can be achieved.

If you cannot stickhandle objections you are unlikely to achieve your stated goals; by caving in when the going gets a little rough, you demonstrate weakness. If you cannot explore difficult objections and situations you will not be an effective advocate for your client. Neither your own organization nor your client will benefit if you cannot stickhandle around the objection.

Imagine a client placing an order for expensive instrumentation components. The time frame for delivery is 90 days, but something changes and the client phones to ask for delivery in 75 days. Will you be able

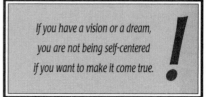

If you have a vision or a dream, you are not being self-centered if you want to make it come true.

to fight for this client? You can be an effective advocate only if you are tenacious. Giving up on objections too easily could be taken as an indication that you will also give up on solving problems. Being nice and supportive, without the ability to ask for the contract, is an indication that you may be ineffective when you must ask your operations manager for something more to meet a client's needs.

Accepting Feedback

There are three attitudes that characterize most salespeople:

1. Some can't; they don't.
2. Some can; they do.
3. Some can't; they do anyway.

Which attitude do you have? Make sure you find out what you don't know about your own attitudes and skills. Be open to receiving help from external sources, from those who observe you and are willing to help you pinpoint areas that need improvement. Truly effective professionals don't hesitate to look for new resources to help them achieve their goals.

Anticipate Objections

During my years of consulting with sales teams, I have consistently asked sales managers and their sales reps for a list of the objections they typically receive. Few of the sales teams I've worked with have completed the relatively simple task of keeping such a list. To be successful, salespeople need to reflect upon past experiences to identify client objections. *How can salespeople respond effectively to objections if the objections have not been identified, and appropriate responses have not been prepared?*

Following is a list of some of the most common individual, internal hurdles, blocks and barriers—due to personality, learned behavior or psychological type—for not having a system in place for handling objections.

Internal Barriers to Receiving Objections

- Salespeople prefer not to know the typical objections they might encounter so they can remain in an elevated state of tension and fear, which makes them feel more animated.

- Salespeople believe motivational speakers and authors who assert that we must all be positive thinkers, and thus they regard anticipation of objections as negative thinking. This is just plain wrong! The penchant for positive thinking, without grounding in reality, will keep a salesperson stuck in mediocrity and doomed to become *a happy underachiever*.

- Salespeople are generally unwilling to take responsibility for keeping a list of typical objections.

- Salespeople don't realize that if customers do not offer any objections, they are not likely to earn the sale. If customers aren't sufficiently involved and engaged to offer objections, they're not likely to be interested in discussing the pros and cons of the product or service.

- Salespeople are unaware that client objections are one means by which a prospect can sort wheat from chaff or goats from sheep. A sales representative who cannot handle a few objections will probably not be able to deal with difficult after-sale concerns.

- Salespeople do not realize how easy it is to handle objections smoothly.

- Salespeople have a low tolerance for discomfort and see objections as an expression of personal disapproval. Taking everything personally is an immature emotional response.

- Salespeople have a tendency to be neurologically "twitchy." They are unable to stay with the process and often want to conclude it prematurely. Sometimes, however, the sales process is long and convoluted.

- Salespeople do not realize that good decision-makers go through a period of due diligence. Instead of becoming intimidated or impatient with the time it takes clients to become comfortable, salespeople could learn to help the client through the process. This will contribute to customer loyalty.

- Salespeople cannot/will not see themselves as consultants. Consultants want to uncover problems and find solutions for the long term. Most sales reps just want a short-term deal.

Complete Your Own Inventory of Objections

There are only six commonly occurring industry objections that clients employ to dissuade you from attempting to secure an appointment. A list of these objections is presented in Chapter 12. Take a moment now, though, to compile a personal inventory of the objections you consistently receive. What objections do your customers give you?

The following exercise will assist you in making an inventory of the objections and situations you face on a regular basis.

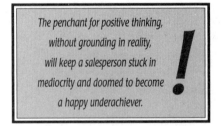

The penchant for positive thinking, without grounding in reality, will keep a salesperson stuck in mediocrity and doomed to become a happy underachiever.

Objections & Situations Inventory

Identify the top three objections you receive from your prospects about your product or service.

1. _____

   _____

2. _____

   _____

3. _____

   _____

List three examples of difficult or confusing situations that arise with your customers. These situations leave you feeling frustrated and wishing you had a better response.

1. _____

   _____

2. _____

   _____

3. _____

   _____

Chapter 2

Internal Objections that Sabotage Success

S INCE THE MIND IS THE MOST POWERFUL TOOL WE HAVE, it is unfortunate that we use it to create objections that undermine our own success. *I think, therefore I am* can become a self-fulfilling prophecy. We need to "scan" our thoughts and "upgrade" them when our concepts are no longer appropriate, do not work, or are out of date.

If we think of our mind in terms of a computer, the memory (hardware) and operating system/applications (software) must work together in order to accomplish some discernible result. In addition, the mind, like a computer, is subject to virus attacks. However, the mind is rarely provided with a software update or upgrade and is also vulnerable to "viruses." Just as we regularly upgrade the memory and software in our computers, we also need to upgrade outdated modes of thinking and behaving that prevent us from being successful. One aspect of our thinking that requires our regular attention and revision, or upgrade, occurs whenever we fall into *Analysis Paralysis*.

Just as a physical paralysis prevents forward movement, so does mental paralysis. Our mind tells us all sorts of dark stories and tales of gloom and doom. Filled with anxiety arising from past failures, we overwhelm ourselves with countless questions and negative thoughts and bring those into our current situation. We begin to believe the mind's propaganda and we become stuck in a quagmire of self-doubt, fear, and insecurity.

Fortunately, you have the power to overcome *Analysis Paralysis*. Do not believe everything you think. Buying into your own insecurities can be a costly venture!

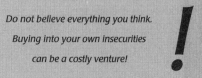

Do not believe everything you think. Buying into your own insecurities can be a costly venture!

Internal Objections

We must work hard to overcome the following internal objections:

1. **Faulty Assumptions**: Every success or failure begins with our assumptions about who we are and what we do. If our assumptions are optimistic, then our actions will likely be proactive, thereby creating positive results. Since every cloud contains a benefit, it is important to ask yourself: *What treasure did I discover from this experience?* Then, remind yourself: *I can become richer by embracing both positive and negative outcomes.*

2. **Unrealistic Expectations of Others**: Are you expecting your carefully cultivated contact to carry your message to the economic decision maker? Have you abdicated your power to someone else? If your contact fails to do as you expect, and you lose the deal, do not hold that person responsible. When you fail to go to the appropriate decision maker, you are the victim of your own failure, not theirs.

3. **Poor Appearance**: A shine on your shoes is a smile on your feet. Looking disheveled will not engender confidence in you on the part of the client. Appearing in the proper attire is the answer, because you get only one chance to make a first impression. Even with hard work, you may not be able to erase a negative first impression.

4. **Language**: Imagine how clients feel if, after they express a concern, you say: *No, you don't understand.* This response places the blame on the client, implying the client has both a listening and a comprehension problem. Instead, you could say: *Perhaps I'm not being clear. Let me put it another way.* A client expects you to be an expert who can provide information using the proper technical terms. Avoid referring to your product as *stuff*, and avoid using the repetitive terms *right, sure, um, ah*. If you use

vague terminology, clients are unlikely to purchase your product or buy your solution to their problems.

5. **Body Language**: It's not just the words we say or how we say them: our body language also makes a difference. For example, arms folded over the chest area sends a message that you are closed—unwilling to listen and perhaps feeling defensive. Closed body posture connotes *nothing out, nothing in.*

6. **Severe Shyness**: Shy people tend to be self-conscious and worried about the impression they are making. One solution for shyness is to focus on the customer by asking questions. You will appear interested, caring, and outgoing, and feel less self-conscious. If practiced daily, this coping skill will become second nature to you. As your shyness dissipates it will be replaced with confidence and success.

7. **Lack of Enthusiasm**: People do not fail because of what they do not know; they fail because they are not enthusiastic about what they *do* know.

8. **Hanging on to a Dead Prospect**: Let unpromising leads go to the competition. As Kenny Rogers sang in his song *The Gambler*, "You gotta know when to hold 'em, know when to fold 'em, know when to walk away, and know when to run..."

9. **Talking and Telling Too Much**: The 80/20 Rule is as good as gold! By allowing your customers 80% of the air time in a conversation, you learn more about their wants, needs, desires and concerns. You contribute to the conversation by asking questions and responding to the customer's queries.

10. **Criticizing the Competition**: If you mention competitors by name, you are advertising for them. If you try to look big by making others look small, you will end up losing the account.

11. **Failing to Manage the Sales-Call Process**: It is a mistake to push the client to get an answer—any answer—rather than understand the due-diligence process your client must follow. Some sales reps would rather push with a hard close and get a *no* than proceed carefully and wait for the answer.

12. **Perfectionism**: *I can't because... or I should but... or What if...?* As discussed in Chapter 1, when we allow doubts to dictate our thoughts we find ourselves in a state of *Analysis Paralysis.* Perfectionists repeat only that which they already know how to do. Show me a perfectionist and I will show you a procrastinator.

> *Perfectionists repeat only that which they already know how to do. Show me a perfectionist and I will show you a procrastinator.*

They avoid attempting other tasks that might challenge their knowledge and skill level or cause them to make a mistake. Perpetual self-doubt encourages us to return to the same experience time and time again and dwell on what we did poorly. The successful salesperson turns past failures into a positive process by finding ways to neutralize the client's objections and make them the juice of future sales.

13. **Not Giving Yourself Choices**: Whenever you tell yourself you should be doing something else, you are actually attempting to browbeat yourself into a higher level of performance. A successful salesperson knows that providing clients with choice can secure a sale. Why do these same individuals fail to recognize their own need for choice and continue to chastise themselves with the word *should*?

Replacing Analysis Paralysis

When faced with a list of names to cold-call or objections to handle, most people experience a number of questions of self-doubt. Here are some of the most common:

- *What if...she snaps at me?*
- *What if...he has a supplier that he's already happy with?*
- *What if...I feel scared or nervous?*
- *What if...they ask me a question and I don't know the answer?*
- *What if...I look foolish?*

The most valuable questions are those we ask clients, not the ones we ask ourselves. *What if* questions tend to paralyze the self-doubters and they become victims of their own design. When we ask ourselves *What if* questions, we are actually being self-centered. If we ask these questions of others, we can become other-centered. The old saying: *No one cares how much you know until they know how much you care*, applies to the sales industry. Asking the client relevant questions is an easy way to show that we care.

If you are to understand someone else's needs and desires, begin the majority of your questions with the words: *What about...?* and *What if...?* This will cause customers to be reflective, to be aware of needs they didn't know they had. In return, they will be more receptive to you and your product or service.

Analysis of your customer's needs creates forward movement and a momentum that fuels the sales process. Critical, judgmental self-analysis leads to self-doubt and self-defeating behaviors and causes *Analysis Paralysis.*

So What?

The question that can release you, the salesperson, from Analysis Paralysis is: *So what?* You may not have all the answers, but you can learn from your experiences and build an arsenal of information for future use. When you have the information, approach the client again, regardless of your earlier doubt or error.

When you are processing an order for your client you may determine that you missed something that was of vital importance. You may find yourself saying: *Oh no, I forgot to ask about _____ !* If this is so, just say to yourself: *So what? At least I know most of the information now and I'll be able to do better next time.* Review the conversation to determine what

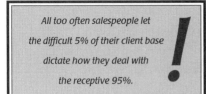

All too often salespeople let the difficult 5% of their client base dictate how they deal with the receptive 95%.

you actually forgot, then call the client to request the additional information.

Suppose your client wants to purchase 100 chairs and you wrote down the quantity, colors and models. When you return to the office, you realize that you didn't ask when the client needed them delivered. *So what?* Instead of beating yourself up over the omission, take the proactive step of calling the client and asking for confirmation of the delivery date.

In another situation, you might encounter a harsh rebuttal when attempting to understand the client's concerns. *So what?* This is not a hit on your character. It's the result of a client having difficulties dealing with issues caused by his own situation. Others will appreciate your empathy even if one client reacted negatively. All too often salespeople let the difficult 5% of their client base dictate how they deal with the receptive 95%.

Failing is Part of the Process

If you practice an honest appraisal of your mistakes, you will learn what you need to do. It's amusing to hear someone say: *It's okay to make a mistake. Just don't make the same one twice.* It's not only okay to make mistakes, it is okay to repeat the same mistake if you still need to learn. One of the most powerful learning tools we have is repetition with purpose.

When people fail or make a mistake, their minds play tricks on them as a means of protection and self-defense. These defenses include denial, the classic response to loss. As adults we seem unable to grieve fully about our losses, even those that are necessary, so there exists within us a small element of anger over those losses—anger that seeks to blame and shame ourselves and others. The next step is denial of our own failures and laying blame on the competition, the economy, or the boss. That is the coward's way.

The courageous way is to accept complete responsibility for results. The spin-off from this more mature response is that by accepting responsibility you begin to see the solution more clearly and more quickly. To help you get through this process, say to yourself: *this too shall pass.* These four words also apply to a long winning streak. Nothing lasts forever!

It is perfectly normal to feel fear. One source of fear is worry, such as worrying about the future. When we assume we'll be worse off in the future than we are now, we need to remind ourselves: *I am safe; it's only change.*

Go ahead. Let your response to failure include experiencing your feelings. Then face the challenge of getting back on track. If you stay stuck in feelings of loss and anger, they will eventually become a quagmire of pessimistic thinking.

It is important to be able to admit to yourself the naked truth. The truth may hurt, but it is only a temporary hurt. When you put an action plan in place to work with your weaknesses, the internal saboteurs slink away and your true potential is free to surface.

Many people wait around hoping that time will sort out their personal problems and that success will be the eventual result. It doesn't happen that way. Results are based on our actions and results provide an enhanced or diminished image of self.

The universe is organized around—and rewards—action. One mentor used to say to me: *there is no point in praying if you don't take action!*

Many salespeople move from one company to another, taking their weaknesses with them. It is better to acknowledge a weakness and take action to correct it than to hope timing, luck or the next job will hold the solution.

Harvest Your Weaknesses

I use the term *harvesting weaknesses* because, just as a farmer harvests his crops for profit, you can harvest your weaknesses for profit. Initially it is painful to face your dark side—your weaknesses and fears—but your potential lies in taking action and transforming weaknesses; see Fig. 1.

By the time we are in our late 20s or early 30s, our achievements will have required us to utilize most of our natural talents. Few people realize that our weaknesses are also a source of potential strength and success.

Successful people monitor their progress and then change as needed. They have the *Leveraging Power of Many.* They can hire an assistant,

Figure 1: Harvesting Weaknesses.

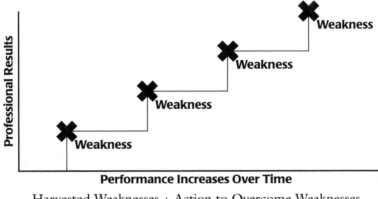

We must understand this before we can climb the steps of consolidation.

Harvested Weaknesses + Action to Overcome Weaknesses
= Improved Professional Results

teach her/him what they know, and double or even quadruple their success. They regularly tap into the power of a little-known secret—their fears and weaknesses—and when confronted, these can be converted into strengths. Unacknowledged weaknesses can and will sabotage even the best of intentions. Successes in early life are usually achieved by drawing upon our natural strengths and talents. Continued success depends upon building a bridge of unity between our strengths and weaknesses.

When a weakness is identified and a plan of action is consistently implemented, a new strength emerges. Successful salespeople are quite familiar with this process. They know that anything worth having is going to cause a certain amount of pain. To think otherwise is to be naive.

Following is a list of common weaknesses which may influence your future success in sales. Check those that apply to you and add any other weaknesses you have.

Common Weaknesses That Sabotage Success

❏ When confronted, I justify and defend my behaviors and myself.

❏ I have poor questioning skills.

❏ I have poor listening skills.

❏ I am inconsistent with time management.

❏ I am moody, prone to self-pity and tend to resent others.

❏ I want to increase my sales yet I avoid cold calling and prospecting.

❏ I am uncomfortable with silence and talk too much.

❏ I am not able to express myself in writing.

❏ I am a people-pleaser. I need to be liked and so, to avoid confrontation, I over-promise.

❏ I don't follow up and consequently lose opportunities.

❏ I am unable to clearly communicate my intentions, ideas, and direction to my team, clients and myself.

❏ I am terrified of public speaking; my presentation skills are less than professional.

❏ I am unable to be assertive and I lack self-confidence.

Case Study: Transforming Weaknesses

Jane described herself as someone who was bright yet under-educated, ambitious but under-performing—according to what she believed her core potential to be. Jane attended my workshop, *Everything You Want is on the Other Side of Fear*, which is about learning strategies to transform fear into courage, and courage into focused action.

During the workshop, she sat near the front and appeared to be highly agitated. I approached her during the break and asked how she was doing. She saw my inquiry as permission to vent, and vent she did. There was something about her, a desperation to move forward, combined with a sincere desire to do the work, that led me to invite her to lunch. There was insufficient time during the break to coach, teach or guide her to the transformation she clearly desired.

The following is a description of the process of change and acceptance of personal weaknesses that Jane experienced. Jane now has her own very successful company, including a condominium rental business catering to international clientele. Among her clients are a number of movie stars.

By the end of our first meeting, we had identified five key fears, and the weaknesses inherent in them, that she wanted to transform:

1. **Fear of confrontation**, which presented itself as her inability to control her emotions and feelings. Whenever an employer or a peer confronted her—or if she suspected criticism—she became defensive and struck out as a protective measure. She could identify and discuss the effects of this pattern on her life but she felt powerless to change. She agreed that she needed to develop her communication skills as well as her ability to manage her feelings and emotions.

2. **Fear of insufficient time** was a big hurdle because she was embarking on these life changes in her early fifties. She felt this transformation was the work of a much younger person.

3. **Fear of economic insecurity** made her feel she should take a job, any job, rather than invest time in herself to discover her true abilities and pursue her passions.

4. **Fear of rejection** was dismantling her because she used up too much energy trying to get people to approve of her. When people told her their truth, if it wasn't what she wanted to hear, she felt disapproval from them. Consequently, she avoided situations where she might experience disagreement. (She now knows the difference between disagreement and disapproval.)

5. **Fear of objections** caused her to feel she had to offer a brilliant comment or risk looking foolish. As a result, she became tongue-tied whenever she encountered the slightest objection.

Jane's willingness to explore these fears (weaknesses) and put a focused action plan in place became the bedrock upon which her new life began to flourish.

Each weakness needed to be explored on many levels because it expressed itself in multiple areas of her life. Fear of rejection showed up when she was dealing with corporate executives. The feelings of anxiety would become so strong that she'd either become tongue-tied in their presence or talk too much! She overcame this weakness by debriefing with me after every important appointment and exploring what she could do differently on the next occasion. She was completely open to scrutinizing her intentions, her hidden agenda, and the exact words and phrases she had used during the appointment.

Jane would take my direction and that of other professional experts, and practice the strategies developed to fit the occasion. It was a privilege to witness her commitment to implementing the principles she'd learned and integrate new responses into her personality in the process. Her expertise in business development continued to grow in direct proportion to her willingness to uncover one weakness after another. Concurrent with this weakness discovery process was her strength recovery process. The ability to seek out experts and ask for help is one of the core strengths that she readily acknowledged (asking for help is key to thriving at any level). Another core strength is her ability and willingness to use the advice she received, without defensiveness. The ability to think reflectively in an objective manner helped Jane take an accurate inventory of her established skills and hidden weaknesses. Reaching a professional low can be dismantling for some, but for Jane it was a motivator.

During this process of rapid personal and professional growth, Jane would have periods where her thinking included: *with all that I want to achieve, there just isn't time!* However, there was time, as there always is, for personal and professional growth. It was only a matter of weeks until we were able to track an upward correlation between her personal growth and her career growth. She built quickly upon the lessons she learned, applying them to similar situations. It was then that we knew her change and growth was permanent rather than situational.

Jane still calls me just as frequently but her calls begin with: *Alice, you'll never guess! I just closed this deal with a large company to supply their visiting executives with condominiums,* or: *Alice, guess what! I just bought a $300,000.00 house with no money down!* Jane would never have achieved these sorts of goals if she hadn't been willing to delve into her weaknesses and get to the other side of her fears.

Jane did the work. She was willing to practice five core competencies:

1. to feel uncomfortable in achieving her goals. She paid a price for her success. The price was to move out of her comfort zone again and again.

2. to be imperfect and perform imperfectly in whatever she attempted. (We agreed upon the key principle of personal mastery: If anything is worth doing it is worth doing imperfectly.)

3. to strive to be consistent when implementing her skills.

4. to tap into her desperation to become truly willing to do the work. (She had GOD—the Gift of Desperation—on her side.)

5. to ask for help and to be influenced by others. (This is a sign of mental health and intelligence.)

Jane's desperation was the beginning of our connection and the motivator behind her success. At this point, she became truly teachable and willing to change. Changing caused her to feel uncomfortable but not as uncomfortable as she would have felt if she had continued to deny her fears and weaknesses.

As is true with everyone, time was indeed on her side. Jane's ideas are rejected sometimes but now she manages her emotions and feelings around that. She no longer feels disapproval or dismantled if someone disagrees with her. Instead, she uses that to encourage her contact to tell her more. If someone expresses a difference in opinion, she explores those differences rather than trying to convince the person to think along her lines. In this manner, she uses objections to advance the sale. She continues the process of digging for weaknesses because she knows that behind every weakness is a strength waiting to be transformed.

The One-Percent Solution

By the time we reach our late 20s or early 30s, our strengths have served us well and it is time to leverage our weaknesses. Although the task of tackling our weaknesses seems daunting, contemplating the alternative—remaining stuck—seems even worse.

Ten years from now, whatever we decide to do, we will all be ten years older. Why not use that time to move forward instead of being stuck in a state of remorse, disappointment, and doubt? Why not leverage these feelings to improve our potential gain?

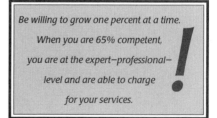

Be willing to grow one percent at a time. When you are 65% competent, you are at the expert–professional–level and are able to charge for your services.

Here is an example of compounding results: *If I offered you a penny a day and promised to double that penny each and every day, would you work for me?* Most people would say no because they don't understand the potential of a penny doubling over time. Allowing yourself to improve one-percent at a time has the same potential—when applied to your earning power.

Cash Value of a Transformed Weakness

Discovering and embracing our weaknesses, without judgment, becomes a point of power. When we begin an action plan to overcome our weaknesses, we begin laughing all the way to the bank.

Be willing to grow one percent at a time. When you are 65% competent, you are at the expert—professional—level and are able to charge for your services. As your competencies increase, you are able to charge more for your services. As demand for your expertise grows, you develop even more areas of competence. As your competence grows so does your internal sense of *benevolent* personal power. It all started with one percent!

Chapter 3

How to Manage Emotions & Feelings

THERE ARE TYPICALLY ONLY SIX OBJECTIONS SPECIFIC TO ANY SECTOR of the sales industry. *Do you know the specific objections for your sector of the sales industry?* If you don't, then you are not functioning as effectively as you might. This chapter is intended to help you manage your emotions and feelings so you are better equipped to identify these objections and, in the process, learn to use them to increase your sales.

Think about a good friend who drops by to visit. Usually you feel excited and pleased, even if the friend comes at an inconvenient time. Your stress level is minimal or nonexistent. Receiving and handling objections can be just as stress free.

Question: *Why don't salespeople make friends with customer objections and be prepared for them?*

Answer: *Fear!*

People who are more inclined to passivity than action will continue to convince themselves not to push the client for a deeper understanding of the objection. They will not ask enough questions and so will be ill equipped to understand the underlying issues and concerns of the client which, if pursued, could lead to a clearer and more appropriate resolution of the problem. Many salespeople don't seek the root of the objection by asking for more details, nor do they explore it by asking questions because they really do not want to know the answers. *Why bother asking?*

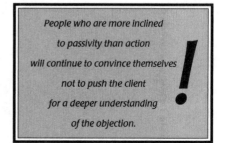

People who are more inclined to passivity than action will continue to convince themselves not to push the client for a deeper understanding of the objection.

Six Quick Steps to Handling Objections!

1. Be receptive to objections.

2. Know all the objections that you will likely receive.

3. Develop a good language/script for handling anticipated objections.

4. Be prepared to feel uncomfortable and to perform imperfectly.

5. Implement your system anyway, even with all of its imperfections.

6. Continually solicit or try to uncover new objections.

If salespeople don't know how to handle the objection, they will avoid seeking it in the first place. This is another example of fear. You can increase your understanding by knowing the probable objections and having a reasonable response. This will decrease your resistance to receiving objections. Imagine that!

The Root of the Problem

When salespeople hear an objection, query or concern, they usually hear it as a problem and rush in to provide an immediate solution—or they perceive it as a rejection of themselves and beat a hasty retreat. These quick responses are rarely effective because there is no understanding of the root cause of the problem. Those feeling fear will fail to ask questions in an attempt to fully understand the basis for the objection. The client has presented an objection for a reason and it is the responsibility of the salesperson to uncover the underlying issues and concerns of the client.

The true extent of a client's problem is contained in and discovered by examining the root of the problem, not by focusing on the symptoms. Imagine going to a doctor because you have a sore foot. The doctor treats the symptom but fails to remove a sliver of glass stuck in your heel.

Temporary relief has been provided but the problem has not gone away. Anxiety and/or fear will cause the salesperson to focus on their own feelings rather than the issues associated with the objection.

Managing Emotions and Feelings

The first step to achieving success is to develop the ability to manage your emotions and feelings. That is not to say you must be without feelings and emotions; it means you manage them instead of letting them manage you. Think of a dog wagging its tail. Now think of the tail wagging the dog. That is how effective your sales activities will become if you do not acknowledge and then transform your feelings of fear, doubt, and insecurity.

Feeling unsafe is valid, but the amount of trepidation you feel when making a cold call may not be an appropriate response, considering the client is not a threat to your physical self. The enormous anxiety is out of proportion and is therefore undermining your performance.

Unless you develop the ability to live with ambiguity and uncomfortable feelings, you will want to avoid anything that makes you feel anxious, but you will languish under the burden of your sensibilities. As a result, your life experiences will be limited.

The primary step in managing your feelings and emotions when you deal with clients (or indeed anyone) is to be willing to feel uncomfortable. The most successful people I know are those who can live with the constant feelings of unease in their chest or gut. When most people feel uneasy, they presume it was the situation or the other person who made them feel that way. You have probably heard someone say: *You make me feel so upset!* The next response from those who cannot manage their feelings of anxiety is often to lash out and attack the person who triggered or activated the feelings. Their defensive response is to say/ think: *You make me feel bad.* This is an example of projection where the person feels uncomfortable feelings and pressure due to

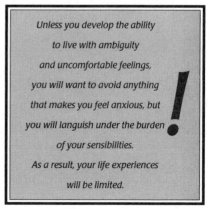

Unless you develop the ability to live with ambiguity and uncomfortable feelings, you will want to avoid anything that makes you feel anxious, but you will languish under the burden of your sensibilities. As a result, your life experiences will be limited.

the confrontation and then blames the person for their reaction to that confrontation.

When you feel upset around someone you could ask yourself: *What is it about me that gets so activated by him/her?* or, *What is it about me that predicts awful consequences when I think about cold calling or public speaking?* When you recognize a pattern of becoming emotionally hooked to people and situations, you can do some advance planning and develop a strategy for responding elegantly to difficult situations.

The second step is to tell yourself a higher story about what is happening and the feelings you have attached to the situation or person. If you change your thinking from negative to realistic—without the awful consequences—that is a miracle. Miracles like this are not difficult to experience, they just requires a change in perception.

> *The next time you feel irritated by a situation or a person, view it as an opportunity to develop a mastery over your emotions and feelings.*

When you search for a higher story, you can usually find something about the situation that can teach you a lesson or cause a degree of enlightenment, no matter how small. When you become consistent at this, you are developing your own *Personal Mastery Life Plan.* Instead of being a victim of your unmanaged emotions and feelings, you have learned to master them. Life shows up with opportunities in the form of vexations just so we can rise above them! It could be said that life works out in the process of life itself.

The next time you feel irritated by a situation or a person, view it as an opportunity to develop a mastery over your emotions and feelings. When you have the opportunity to elevate your perceptions, feel grateful, for you are raising your level of *Personal Mastery.*

Three factors contributing to under-performance are:

1. An inability to tolerate feelings of discomfort.

2. The desire to perform perfectly.

3. Inconsistent implementation of a system.

An average plan implemented often is better than an outstanding plan implemented only on occasion.

This is a transcription of a conversation I had with the vice-president of a national bank:

VP:	"After you work with my team, I want them all to feel confident."
Alice:	"When the president of this bank calls you into his office and asks you to head up a new initiative, would you say: *but Mr. President, I'm not confident in that area.*"
VP:	"Of course not. I'd get busy and learn what I needed to learn."
Alice:	"Exactly. Isn't it their ability to manage uncomfortable feelings that you really want from your team?"
VP:	With a look of understanding dawning on his face, "Of course—the ability to proceed while feeling fear and uncertainty."
Alice:	"Good. I will leave them with that ability."

Confidence is good as far as it goes, but it doesn't go far enough. What is more important is the ability to take action while feeling insecure. The power and potency of a person is unleashed when fear, doubt and insecurity visit but do not dominate.

Three Key Components To Success

The most successful people are those who:

1. Are willing to feel uncomfortable. They know that to be above average, they must move out of their comfort zone. They weigh the probability of long-term gain against short-term discomfort, and choose to move ahead anyway.

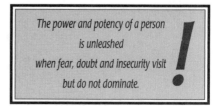

The power and potency of a person is unleashed when fear, doubt and insecurity visit but do not dominate.

2. Do not have the need to always execute a perfect performance. They do not

think: *What if I make mistakes and other people find out?* or, *I want to be seen only in a positive way, so I'll wait until I can do it perfectly.* Successful people have developed the ability to work despite feeling insecure and uncomfortable. Moreover, they are willing to make mistakes.

3. Know that consistent effort is everything. The power of improving one-percent now, consistently, day after day, is compounded when they are willing to do the best they can in the moment. Unfortunately, many people postpone indefinitely what needs to be done now because they want to leave the starting gate not as a beginner, but with a veteran's ease and ability. Realistically, everyone who accepts a new challenge stumbles. Only true veterans look smooth.

You want to do it perfectly? Get over it! Sixty-five percent is a critical mass of competence, raising you to the professional level where you can charge for your services.

Remember Neil Diamond's song?

On the Way to the Sky

We pity the poor one
The shy and unsure one
Who wanted it perfect
And waited too long.

Chapter 4

The Hazards of Perfectionism

REMEMBER PETER FALK IN *COLUMBO*? He consistently implemented a system of apparent ineptitude: "But I still don't understand.... Could you please explain to me one more time, if x is like this and y is like that, then how could z occur?" Colombo's ineptitude was a well-disguised operating system called a *Mastery Program*, one of two common approaches to gathering information and learning.

By analogy, we could compare these two approaches to an audio recording. We'll call one approach the A-side. A few people are born with this ability and they are indeed fortunate. People operating with a *Mastery Program* are willing to make mistakes and in fact believe that mistakes are an important ingredient in their success. They don't need everything to be perfect in order for them to learn, undertake and implement a new process.

Individuals who practice a *Mastery Program* do have difficult times, and when a difficult situation arises, they draw upon hard-won knowledge and experience. Those who focus on developing mastery are quick to ask for help and are willing to admit when they don't know the answer. They do not feel shame for their lack of knowledge. When they see team members struggling with tasks, they are likely to come to their aid. They do not judge others, but instead offer assistance and guidance and, perhaps more importantly, if a mistake has been made, *they believe they made it!*

In contrast, on the B-side of the record is the *Perfectionist Program*. People operating from this *program believe they are the mistake.* Since perfectionists are unforgiving and overly critical of themselves, they tend to be less flexible and less tolerant of others. People

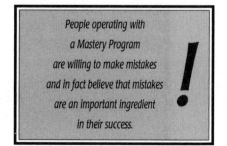

People operating with a Mastery Program are willing to make mistakes and in fact believe that mistakes are an important ingredient in their success.

adopting this approach need to learn to let go one percent at a time. Perfectionists usually have great initial intentions but these rarely translate into action and, when success is not as great as they hoped for or is slow in coming, their resolve dwindles. Figures 2 and 3 show the upward growth and success curves of each approach.

Perfectionist Program

A great idea is born *but* perfectionists don't immediately have all the facts. They're caught up in *Analysis Paralysis* and hope someone will show up and discover their brilliance. They may see the person in the *Mastery Program* (who is actually less skilled) succeeding where they would fail. The result of this perceived injustice means perfectionists tend to judge the world as an unfair place, where people who do not strive for perfection are rewarded more handsomely. They gather thoughts of resentment and blame as comfort.

Figure 2: Perfectionist Program.   **Figure 3: Mastery Program.**

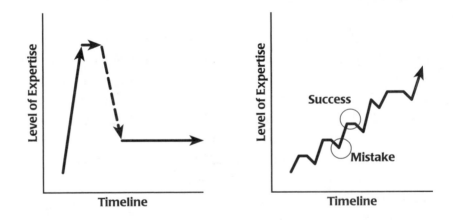

Mastery Program

They begin with an idea, a vision and one percent ability, knowing that expertise will develop along the way.

The Comfort Zone

The truth is, you will not be comfortable when you first try a new system. You will desperately want to scurry back to your comfort zone, or, to phrase it more aptly, to a familiar zone of discomfort. It's natural for you to feel this way; most people do. Actually getting out there without all the skills, even when you feel anxiety and trepidation, is easier in the long run than watching those who are less competent charm the clients, close the deals, and move to the top of the pack.

After surgery, the sensation of your skin healing is quite uncomfortable. Forming new habits feels like that. Everyone who tries new techniques or systems feels uncomfortable, artificial—and maybe even a little manipulative—until the new processes are integrated into their skill set. This is the time to be willing to live with and manage your uncomfortable feelings. The best way to integrate new behaviors is to practice a process called *overlaying*.

Overlaying (Integrating) New Behavior

Overlaying involves practicing a new behavior repeatedly until the negative feelings about the behavior disappear. This is an approach used by *Toastmasters International* to help people overcome their fear of public speaking. The Ice Breaker speech provides the perfect introduction to making speeches, as it asks the speaker to prepare a five-minute presentation on an easy topic—the speaker himself. Gradually, a speaker will advance to assignments that are more complicated and it is during this process that fear begins to dissipate. However, the feelings of fear never completely leave the speaker. In fact, it is the harnessing of this fear that provides the fuel and enthusiasm for making future presentations.

Firewalkers have been asked to share the secret of being able to walk barefoot across red-hot coals. Their answer may shock you. They say the reason they can walk across red-hot coals is because they never lose their nervousness. One physiological reaction to feeling nervous is perspiration or sweating, which is what actually saves a firewalker's feet from being blistered. The day the firewalker loses his fear is the day that he will either abandon the process or will find alternative ways to make his feet sweat before walking on red-hot coals.

Overcome the Fear of Cold Calling

One of the methods I use to desensitize a salesperson's fear of cold calling is described in my book, *Prospect & Prosper: Cold Calling Strategies for the Feint of Heart!* I call it the *256 Cold Call Rule*. During this process, the fear of cold calling dissipates at a predictable rate. Here's how it works.

You begin with your intention to become willing to cold call. You list this intention under the heading "Business Activities Designed to Help Me Become Successful." Since there are 256 shades of gray between black and white, that is as good a number as any for the number of cold calls you need to make before you become comfortable with the process. This number is simply a way to show that overcoming the fear of cold calling is an incremental process. Overcoming a fear is not something that can be done in a single step or one fell swoop.

In the overlay process, you make one cold call at a time. With each call, you observe your thoughts and emotional responses, your willingness to call and your tendencies to procrastinate. Soon the fear begins to slip away until only a small proportion remains. You need to maintain and hold onto 20% of your fear if you want continued success. Without fear there is no courage, and courage is the active ingredient that fuels motivation. Motivation means the willingness to feel the pain and pay the price in order to meet our goals.

This concept of overlaying came to me as I listened to a tape by Deepak Chopra in which he explains that all people would have more success in their careers and their relationships if they gave up justifying and defending their actions or lack of action. When I heard Chopra say this, I had an epiphany and I was never the same again. I totally and absolutely stopped justifying and defending! I began to ask myself questions such as:

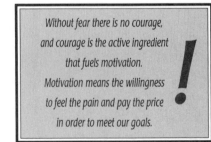

Without fear there is no courage, and courage is the active ingredient that fuels motivation. Motivation means the willingness to feel the pain and pay the price in order to meet our goals.

- *Why am I not making these calls?*
- *Why do I always seem to be let down by others?*
- *Why did I miss out on this deal?*
- *Why do people like that upset me?*

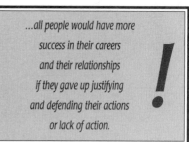

...all people would have more success in their careers and their relationships if they gave up justifying and defending their actions or lack of action.

I consistently overlaid personal ownership, or *Personal Mastery* questions such as these, to any situation over which I did not have full mastery. When you ask yourself these types of ownership questions you begin to take complete responsibility for yourself. Your whole life will be transformed as you become a more empowered person.

Yes, I still feel insecure and uncomfortable when I am confronted by the unfavorable opinions of others, by the objections of prospects, by making certain prospecting calls or by being aggressively held accountable for my own actions. However, I do not react defensively. Instead, I usually respond with this three-step process:

Step 1: *Tell me more!*

Step 2: *Thank you for sharing that with me. I appreciate the feedback.*

Step 3: *Is there anything else you'd like to reveal to me about that?*

This reaction did require a few repetitions before I was able to unhook emotionally from confrontation, but eventually the overlaying did the trick.

Justifying and Defending is No Way to Grow

When faced with an objection or personal critique, some salespeople move into a series of rationalizations. The preferred response is to ask a question about the expressed concern, remembering to allow time for the person to respond to your question. You appear to be genuinely interested by showing courtesy and respect.

You always know if you are justifying and defending by the words you use to begin your sentences:

- *Ya, but...*
- *But it's different for you...*
- *It's easy for him/her. But for me...*
- *I can't because...*
- *However...*
- *This wouldn't work for me...*
- *Ya, well, she deserved it because...*
- *I already know that...*

There was no justification for not handling objections before you began reading this book. Now that you have it in your hands, there is definitely no excuse or defense for not being able to handle objections. You now have guidelines to help you deal with *no*.

Chapter 5

The Confidence Myth

EVERY BUSINESSPERSON WISHES CLIENTS WOULD BE EASIER TO FIND, develop, and maintain. As human beings, we wish lots of things were easier to accomplish. It is magical thinking to hope someone will come along and rescue us from the difficult aspects of learning and of driving new business. When we understand that it won't get easier, we take courses and read books on how to develop confidence and self-esteem. Guess what? That doesn't work either!

The only path to confidence is through competence. You will feel confident only when you have handled enough objections and questioned enough clients so you can truly understand clients' issues and needs. Confidence follows competence; there is no other path. I wish I could write the book that would enable you to develop confidence; but even if I could, that would deprive you of developing the necessary skills to deal with life on life's terms. Imagine being confident without competence.

Let's look at Figure 4, where we see Jill, who is venturing from her comfort zone. Jill's motivation to do something new is a result of beginning to see her comfort zone as a discomfort zone. When the comfort zone begins to be too uncomfortable, Jill becomes frustrated, depressed, anxious, and begins to doubt herself. She also feels resentment toward her friends and family who are busily fulfilling their dreams. Finally, the pain becomes too much for her, and she is willing to move out of her comfort zone.

Two friends, Jason and Tim, now join her. They are also moving out of their comfort zones, and, for them, fear is also the dominant feeling. Jason, Jill, and Tim feel trepidation, and expect the journey to be hard. Because they have no experience, they have no confidence. Halfway through the learning curve, the going gets tough, and they have a setback. Tim and Jill head directly back to their familiar discomfort zone, while

Figure 4: Confidence develops through Competence.

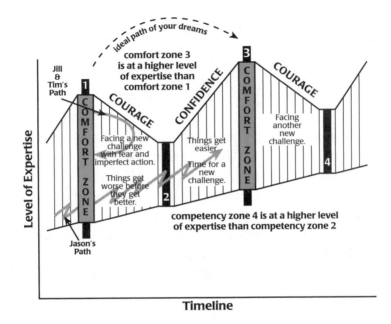

Jason draws upon knowledge and hard won experience, hunkers down and faces the frightening situation directly. For Jason, Tim, and Jill, the uncomfortable feelings are there, yet for Jason, these feelings do not dismantle his resolve. Going back is not an option for him, so Jason struggles ahead imperfectly.

As Jason becomes more competent, what was difficult becomes easier. This is a progressive cycle and each time the cycle is repeated Jason moves to discomforts that are more complex. After a while, the job that caused Jason such angst in the beginning becomes easy, even routine. It becomes part of his comfort zone, which also needs to be dismantled, and again the cycle repeats itself. The constant renewal of competence gives him an air that others perceive as confidence. In reality, it is Jason's inner assurance they perceive. This inner assurance comes from a relationship with hard won experience, not from wishing or listening to inspirational talks.

This relationship with experience provides a solid confidence in one's ability to live through challenging and difficult times. There is no other way—no books, no seminars, and no guru—to achieve confidence except through competence.

Paradoxically, the challenges and difficulties must be experienced before confidence can build and become part of your character. How sad it is that we have come to see self-esteem and confidence as states of grace to be inherited or given, rather than achieved. *Everything You Want is on the Other Side of Fear* is the title of my third book in the GutsGoalsGlory™ series. It outlines a dozen or more common fears, and the path to transforming those fears that otherwise dismantle success.

With more personal resources at his disposal, Jason starts facing new challenges. Each time this cycle repeats, his capacity increases. The desire to feel confident is not part of his mindset. Jason knows that fear, combined with imperfect action, are the main ingredients to courage. Acquiring courage and competence is more practical than seeking supreme self-confidence.

Where would we find the motivation, the drive for excellence and self-protection if we never felt fear? All of us would excel if we could move from our comfort zone and arrive at competence in one easy step. This is simply magical thinking, and to that I say: *In your dreams!*

Traits that helped Jason bridge the gap include:

1. The ability to focus on the desired outcome.
2. The ability to give himself the right to achieve success.
3. The willingness to make mistakes—in order to achieve more success one must be willing to make more mistakes.
4. The ability to ask for help; asking for help is not cheating!
5. Discipline—doing the right thing because it is simply the right thing to do.
6. The willingness to experience uncomfortable feelings.
7. The willingness to accept there is a price to be paid for everything worth having.
8. Detachment: ability to detach from the outcome.

Things Can Get Worse Before They Get Better

When we attempt to learn new skills, and implement new behaviors, the feelings of discomfort often get worse before we begin to feel comfortable. Following each dip or trough, in Figure 4, we experience an increasing sense of confidence which accompanies the realization that we have mastered a new competency.

Do you remember when you learned how to parallel park? You probably made fifty attempts, each one a little better than the last. Then, one day, voila! you parallel parked without a problem. That was the moment in time when you hit the competency zone shown in Figure 4. It probably came unnoticed, but your ability to parallel park was never questioned again. When you tackle new challenges repeatedly, you become competent in new skills, you develop resilience, competence, and only then will you have confidence. You then seek out bigger challenges for bigger and better rewards. You are aware that you are not immune to unscheduled encounters with fear and trepidation, yet you do not organize your life to avoid them. You are willing to face them as they occur—to take life on life's terms.

> *When you tackle new challenges repeatedly, you become competent in new skills, you develop resilience, competence, and only then will you have confidence.*

Courage is the Answer

Self-confidence, whether you have it or not, is now a moot point because you are able to feel uncomfortable and succeed anyway. You are able to combine fear with unconditional action and movement, and it has become part of your familiar routine with your prospects and clients. Because of your journey into the arena of discomfort, it now becomes easier for you to truly hear the concerns, needs, and objections of your client. Your own feelings of comfort can be easily sacrificed to allow your clients to feel confident that you care about their problems and concerns. The results will show!

No Objection Usually Means No Sale

A client who does not make objections might have comforted you before, but now it should strike dread in your heart. As you begin to understand this concept, you'll begin to bring up objections yourself, and to encourage customers to reveal their concerns. You'll even anticipate your customers' concerns and negative responses. Moreover, you'll know that positive thinking without grounding in reality can destroy your business goals. Anticipate objections and prepare responses to them. When they show up, you can receive them as you receive a

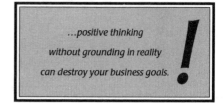

...positive thinking without grounding in reality can destroy your business goals.

good friend dropping in to visit at an inconvenient time. The benefits of having them visit far outweigh any temporary stress.

Please...develop a list of objections and situations that you encounter in your everyday interactions with your prospects and clients. Then match them up with what you discover in this book. If you adopt this advice as part of your system, success will be yours—I promise! If not now, then when?

Too many times in the past, a prospect looked at your proposal and declared it perfect. You confidently included that prospect in your monthly sales forecast, only to be embarrassed at the next sales meeting because you didn't hear from him again. Now you know, as I do, that a customer who gives no objections means *No Sale!*

Develop the skill of objection handling. Every new skill requires a period of learning for the beginner. Becoming receptive to the objections of customers is a prerequisite to success. When you receive the objection, do not begin to talk about it or show panic. It is not a rejection of you, nor are you required to have all the answers. Instead, ask questions to clarify and understand the root of the objection. Above all, don't expect perfection in yourself or in your clients.

Chapter 6

Questions are the Answer, Aren't They?

YOU HAVE BEEN GREETED IN THE LOBBY AND ESCORTED INTO THE BOARDROOM. Now what? The first few minutes of the sales call are, without a doubt, just as uncomfortable for the customer as they are for you, the seller. Fortunately, there is a simple technique to minimize this discomfort. This technique is easy to learn and, if you take the time to master it, you will realize increased sales. That's the purpose of this chapter.

The truly professional salesperson takes charge and effortlessly creates a comfort zone for the client. Creating this comfort zone is possible only if the salesperson has a plan. This plan is presented to the customer in the form of a call objective. Salespeople know it is their job to disarm the client's defenses and pretenses and to make the client receptive to revealing needs and concerns (objections to buying). In fact, the client has probably resolved to not be susceptible to your presentation.

These defenses must be dissolved before you can encourage the prospect to reveal any blocks to buying. Only by redefining and exploring those blocks will you be able to move on to the proposal-writing stage.

Build Your Customer's Comfort Zone

When you first meet with clients, what do you do? What do you say? Remember, it is important to keep your clients in their comfort zone. If they're feeling uncomfortable, they are not feeling good about you. You are a stranger trying to sell to them. You are perceived as the cause of their discomfort.

Creating and promoting a customer comfort zone is vital. The following four steps will help you to achieve just that. This process will assist you in moving towards closure more frequently.

1. **Wear a big, wide smile!** If you show a small child a picture of her unsmiling mother and a picture of a smiling stranger, she will choose to gaze longer at the smiling stranger: smiles are powerful.

2. **Pay your client a compliment.** It doesn't have to be personal; it could be about the company website or the office lobby.

3. **Give a small gift, such as a business magazine.** "My company has several subscriptions to *Fast Company* so I thought I'd bring one along in case you haven't had a chance to pick it up." Although this gift could be considered personal, it is probably acceptable to give in most situations because other people within the client's office are likely to read it too and share in the benefit.

4. **Establish a call objective.** When you inform the customer what you hope to achieve and agree upon, the client will breathe a subconscious sigh of relief. You will have created a framework around the call. You tell the client how much time you'll need, how you will proceed (by asking questions, such as: *Is it alright if I leave here with my facts straight by asking you a few questions today?*) and how the sales process will proceed. Also, be sure to ask clients if there is anything else s/he would like to achieve, or if they want to cover anything in particular.

Create a Call Objective

Call objectives are interim goals that you have to meet in order to achieve the greater goal of closing. Some examples of call objectives are to obtain the information you need, to get names of other players, to learn how purchasing decisions are typically made, or to achieve a letter of intent.

For many reasons, it is necessary to set call objectives. One of the most important is to be able to conduct a self-appraisal at the end of the call. That's when we ask ourselves some difficult *Call to Truth* questions.

- *Did I have a call objective?*
- *What was that objective?*
- *Did I meet my call objective?*
- *Was my call objective realistic?*
- *Who do I need to contact next?*
- *What do I need to do next?*
- *Who can help me?*

Create a Context

A context is the framework, the container that goes around something. For example, imagine a yard that is contained by a fence. That fence creates a context for the property. When we create context with our clients we:

- Review where we are in the process.
- State what your objective, or goal, is for the call.

For example: *Juliet, so far we have met twice, and during those meetings I became much clearer on your company's financial needs. I now understand your requirement for a flexible payment schedule due to fluctuating receivables. What I propose today is for us to go over your foreign exchange requirements and the related issues. Does this sound reasonable to you? Oh yes, before I go I would appreciate a copy of your company's organizational chart so I can better understand how decisions and ideas flow.*

A sales trainer who is meeting with a prospect could establish this call objective with her client: *I understand your company recently purchased a new press at substantial cost and you are keenly interested in using this new press to its full capacity. Is this accurate or am I out in left field with my information?* If the client agrees that you've been correctly informed, you could then say: *What I'd like to do today is discuss with you how I help sales teams significantly increase their business in six months without increasing their hours or effort. First, I need to ask a few questions to understand the sales process currently in place. Is this okay with you? Will you be willing to set another appointment if we go beyond today's allotted time?*

If your client agrees, you can begin your questioning. Your first questions should not be loaded. There should be no negative emotional charge. For example, imagine meeting with the Vice President, Marketing and Sales about her sales team's poor quarterly performance and immediately saying: *So, tell me about the poor performance of your sales team last quarter.* You will need to ask a version of this question sometime during your sales process, but not until you have established some rapport, trust and receptivity with your client.

A few non-loaded questions are necessary to break the ice and to set the stage. I ask my questions in a three-step process.

1. **Bridging Questions (earning the right)**
   There are usually four to eight general questions about your client's business. These are safe to ask because you are building a bridge with your customer. At first, both of you will be slightly uncomfortable, as most of us are, when we meet new people. Your bridging questions could be basic:

   - *How long has your company been in business?*
   - *Have the recent mergers in our city affected your company?*
   - *How does your company stay competitive?*

2. **Questions to Uncover Client's Concerns**
   This series of questions is designed to uncover problem areas. When a problem is identified, go on to another by asking similar questions. However, DO NOT rush in with a solution. When a client complains about a problem and you rush in with a solution, you show how smart and competent you are, but your solution is almost certainly based on only a small part of the whole problem. It also increases the likelihood that the client will feel foolish and become defensive, which tends to dampen any desire to make further disclosures about the key issues. Ask questions about the problem as follows:

   - *Which business issues keep you awake at night?*
   - *What has worked in the past?*

- *What other solutions have you tried?*
- *What would you do if money were not a problem?*

3. **Ramifications of the Main Problem**

   At this stage, your questions should be asked so as to learn more about the main problem. You gently probe the boundaries of the issue, teasing out the ramifications of the main problem. Not many salespeople know this, but people do not make a decision to change because of their problem. They make a decision to change because of the pain and consequences associated with the problem.

Remove the Customer's Blocks to Buying

Discovering a customer's true needs is a complicated process. It involves questioning, listening, repeating what you hear, asking more questions, being just a little bit paranoid, asking more questions and finally, helping the prospect come to the decision that you are indeed a match.

It is okay, and even appropriate, to be just a bit paranoid—do not take the pending sale for granted. Too many have counted their money before the deal was done, having believed their own optimistic thinking rather than asking delicate requalifying questions. That is one of the problems with the positive-thinking philosophies that surround the sales

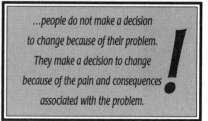

...people do not make a decision to change because of their problem. They make a decision to change because of the pain and consequences associated with the problem.

profession: positive thinking without a grounding in reality leads to happy underachievers!

The salesperson usually makes the decision before the client, that there is a match between his/her product/service and the prospect's needs. Depending on the nature of the sale, the client may lag behind by anywhere from 30 seconds to two years! The gap between the present state of affairs and the anticipated resolution is often an obstacle course full of objections, concerns, and conditions.

From the date of initial client contact to the actual implementation of the sale, there may even be a change in key personnel. A formal *Needs/*

Issues Assessment (Chapter 7) will not only increase your chances of heading off your competitor should a key contact leave or be transferred, but it will help you to be (and appear to be) more conscientious, strategic, organized and logical.

The *Needs/Issues Assessment* is a living, breathing document which changes and evolves as the buying climate changes and evolves. When salespeople have the ability to question and listen, they generally enjoy a good relationship with clients and potential clients; ultimately they reap the financial rewards of those relationships.

A salesperson who functions without the ability to question and listen will not develop a good relationship with clients. The most an unskilled salesperson can hope for is that the competition is less skilled at understanding the client.

The typical salesperson responds to a client's statement of a problem by jumping in with a solution. Talk, talk, talk, tell, tell, tell, explain, explain, explain and solve, solve, solve the problem. Just the opposite reaction is required—*ask questions*. The prospect/client will be grateful if you show a sincere desire to understand their concerns and needs by asking appropriate questions. Think of it this way: wisdom, understanding, and knowledge are fast-tracked by questioning. There are appropriate times to talk and, if you show a sincere desire to understand your client's needs, there will be time to let your client know what you know—not until you are clear on their needs!

When a salesperson responds with a solution based on an understanding of 20% of the problem, the solution will solve only 20% of the problem. There is not much chance of becoming a client's relationship partner with this mode of communication. Who would want a relationship with a person who doesn't understand them? This is not the quality of business relationship your most valued accounts expect from you.

Why don't we ask more questions, not just of our clients, but of friends and family as well? In the course of my own work experience, I have repeatedly encountered the following seven reasons.

The four most dangerous words that any salesperson could utter are: *I already know that*. Those who say this have contempt for exploration. The questioner's paradox, of course, is the only way to know the answers is to ask more questions.

Seven Blocks to Asking Questions

1. **Disinterest**

2. **Self-centeredness**
   - Focus is on my quota, my product, and my performance.
   - Feel we must quickly prove our worth.
   - Interested in preserving our self-image and avoiding failure.
   - Need to be in control.

3. **Bad Habits**
   - Unenlightened self-interest (we have too few friends who tell us what we need to know).

4. **Denial**
   - Do not want to know the answer because that would require taking some responsibility for what was disclosed.

5. **Wounded Questioners**
   - As children we are told not to bother authority figures—children are to be seen but not heard!
   - The education system and schools focus on always having the right answer.

6. **Ignorance**
   - Unaware that questioning gives permission for others to talk
   - Unaware that it is indeed polite to ask questions.

7. **Lack of Skill**
   - Do not know how to ask with elegance and grace
   - Fail to realize that questioning is a learned skill.

Of the seven reasons for not asking questions listed on the previous page, the two I encounter most frequently are ignorance—people believe

Figure 5: Uncovering Client Concerns.

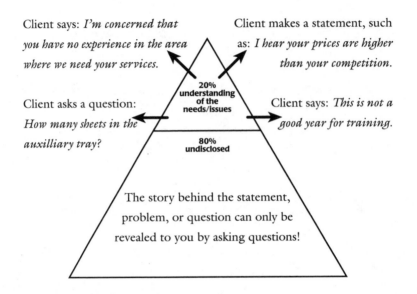

Client says: *I'm concerned that you have no experience in the area where we need your services.*

Client makes a statement, such as: *I hear your prices are higher than your competition.*

20% understanding of the needs/issues

Client asks a question: *How many sheets in the auxilliary tray?*

Client says: *This is not a good year for training.*

80% undisclosed

The story behind the statement, problem, or question can only be revealed to you by asking questions!

that probing with questions is impolite, and lack of skill—people do not know how to ask these questions in a manner that shows respect for others and themselves.

Typical Client/Salesperson Interaction

Client's Action		Salesperson's Reaction
1. Present a problem.	☞	• Immediately offer a solution without seeking elaboration.
2. State a fact.	☞	• Launch into a discussion without further exploration.
3. Ask a question?	☞	• Answer the question without further probing.

To counteract these three typical reactions, I offer the following responses which are all quite easy to learn and apply:

1. When you are presented with a **problem** encourage others to flesh it out by saying: *Could you tell me more about that?*

2. When someone makes a **statement of fact**, practice saying: *Because...?* The results (additional information) will amaze you before you are even halfway through the conversation.

3. When you are asked a **question**, encourage further discussion by saying: *I'm curious. Why do you ask that?* If you introduce a *why* question with *I'm curious*, it makes the question a great deal less confrontational.

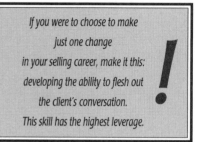

If you were to choose to make just one change in your selling career, make it this: developing the ability to flesh out the client's conversation. This skill has the highest leverage.

Ask Questions to Close More Deals

Understanding the many benefits of questioning and knowing how to encourage easy, simple and respectful responses will guarantee a higher return on your sales effort. *Would you be willing to begin today?* Remember, practice imperfectly instead of waiting for perfection.

Chapter 7

Needs Assessments Resolve Objections

T<small>HE TRADITIONAL METHODS OF HANDLING OBJECTIONS</small> can be combative. A *Needs/Issues Assessment* on the other hand, is a collaborative process accomplished by asking questions and getting agreement to proceed to the next step.

The starting point for anything worth achieving is intention. Whenever you declare your intention, that intention becomes evident in your life. The shadow side of intention is a *hidden agenda*. If your *hidden agenda* is just to get by, to get the most out of life without putting the equivalent back, you will have meager results.

An example of a worthy intention is the search to find something good or high-spirited in all people with whom you are dealing. With some people, that's not easy. It requires very little character to be spiritually elegant with someone who is already kind, sweet, nurturing, and accommodating. The people who challenge our equanimity are actually gifts: they force us to reach deep inside and access our humane resources.

Hidden agendas are often associated with wanting to look smart at someone else's expense: to see someone else fail, to do less than others, or to get even with someone. Often, we are actually projecting frustration from a negative past experience onto a present situation. We didn't settle the score then, so we unconsciously attempt to settle it now. This is known as the 'kick the cat syndrome.'

The answer is to consistently review your intentions. While this may sound simple, it's not easy. A properly executed review requires the ability to discern strengths and weaknesses without harsh judgments. Begin by knowing that your awareness of having a hidden agenda is a slippery slope. In situations where you experience difficulty or conflict, ask yourself tough questions, such as: *Could I be feeling greedy?* Or: *What is it about me that is preventing me from dealing effectively with this person?*

Perhaps you are feeling angry, powerless, or inadequate in one or more areas of your life, and are jealous of someone who appears to have it together in a way that you don't. As a result, you criticize him or her. In this case, the thoughts of judgment are really about yourself, although you're projecting the envy and anger onto someone else.

Scanning your intentions is one key method to fast forward personal growth and self-awareness. Soon you will become aware of the core truth about who you are. You will notice that most of the time you think generously and helpfully about others. Occasionally, you'll notice the opposite and be able to take corrective internal action. If you aren't sure what you're seeing when you scan your intentions, here's a hint: when you scan and find negative intentions, your relationships will probably be negative. Unlike a magnetic field, the energy field that resides within all of us decrees *that like attracts like*—as in the childhood saying: *birds of a feather, flock together.*

If it is your sincere intention to know about your clients' needs so you can help them resolve those needs, then you will want to use this list of seven steps:

1. **State the intention**: *If it's okay with you, I would like to ask a few questions about your needs/requirements.*

2. **State what's in it for the customer**: *What we discover may help us better understand what works for you, and provide a dialogue in which you can express your ideas and concerns.*

3. **Keep a record**: *Is it alright if I take notes? I don't want to miss anything.* (Notice how you have provided a reason why you are taking notes). Write everything down and don't justify, defend, respond or give solutions. See Figure 6 in this chapter.

4. **State what's in it for you**: *I will come to know the issues that positively and negatively affect you. This will help me gain a clearer picture of your unique needs and goals, so that when I leave here I'll have the facts.*

5. **Encourage feedback and ask questions**: *Anything else? What else?* or *What has worked before?*

6. **Create a formal list**: with issues on one side and status/resolution on the other. (See Figure 6, *Needs/Issues Assessment*, p. 74).

7. **Continually develop this process**: by asking three simple questions derived from the following:

   - *What one thing do you want me to keep doing?*
   - *What one thing do you want me to stop doing?*
   - *What one thing do you want me to start doing?*

For different scenarios, you can substitute another word for ME. For example: *What one thing do you want* THE COMPETITION *to keep doing?* or: *What one thing do you wish* THE SALES TEAM *would keep doing?*

It is worth mentioning that the reason for phrasing the question with *What one thing...* is because you don't want the client to draw a blank. A limit of one is easy to figure out because it is definitive. Then you can always ask: *What is one other thing...?*

If you ask a child: *What did you learn at school today?* the usual response is: *Nothing.* However, you would get a better response if you ask: *What one thing did you learn at school today?*

At the next meeting with your client, review the list of issues/needs covered in previous meetings. You will be able to add, delete, or change as appropriate. This may sound tedious, but corporate issues and challenges change daily. You need to know those changes in detail. Don't take anything or anyone for granted.

It helps to complete a *Needs/Issues Assessment* in a formal manner because as you write the information down you are able to add comments or other ideas that will support the client. Another great reason for recording a client's needs and issues is not so you can remember, but so you can forget. You can use your brain to be in the moment of the meeting and review the client's concerns later.

Your *Needs/Issues Assessment* form is a valuable tool to bring to the next meeting. Use it at the beginning of each meeting to review and

Figure 6: Formalize the Needs/Issues Assessment.

Problem	Status/Resolution
1. **Major Presenting Problem**	1. _____
• 1st concern arising from 1…	A. _____
• 2nd concern arising from 1…	B. _____
• 3rd concern arising from 1…	C. _____
2. **Second Presenting Problem**	2. _____
• 1st concern arising from 2…	A. _____
• 2nd concern arising from 2…	B. _____
• 3rd concern arising from 2…	C. _____
3. **Third Presenting Problem**	3. _____
• 1st concern arising from 3…	A. _____
• 2nd concern arising from 3…	B. _____
• 3rd concern arising from 3…	C. _____

recap the previous meeting. You could use a script similar to this: *Before we begin, let's review our last meeting to see if there is anything else you would like to add or discuss in greater detail.*

After you get a response from the client, you will be able to structure the meeting based on his/her latest needs. Instead of using Figure 6, you may choose to draw a circle with satellite circles, as shown in Figure 8, Chapter 8. Either way, record the information for your next meeting, and use it as a template for all your sales calls.

Gently and Tenderly Wounding

Let me explain the concept of *Gently and Tenderly Wounding* your customers when discussing their problems or needs. When a client discloses a problem, a typical salesperson rushes in with a solution. The well-informed salesperson will ask questions and, naturally, the client will feel slightly uncomfortable because sensitive issues and problems are being discussed. However, you must proceed because only when you have a full understanding of the situation can you offer a solution.

As an example, when cold calling a Vice President, Marketing and Sales you might say: *I work with leaders who always intend to spend more time with their sales team but who never seem to find the time to mentor, coach and train them.* Alternatively, you might say: *I support the expectations of a sales leader who wants it done just right, but doesn't have the time to keep this commitment to themselves or their team.*

Acknowledge the intentions of the VP, Marketing and Sales, so it's clear, by your line of questioning, that their actions and intentions do not match. If this is the case, you can say: *I can help your sales team increase their business significantly, without you or them working any harder.* The platform from which to make this statement would not have existed without the VP's answers to your initial probing questions—without gently wounding him or her.

The obstacle that needs to be overcome is our discomfort related to asking questions. It is as if we are hearing adult voices that reinforce behavior learned in childhood.

- *Don't be nosy.*
- *Don't bother the adults.*
- *Children should be seen and not heard.*
- *Who do you think you are? Asking all those questions!*

Remembering those admonishments, we become both wounded questioners and wounded learners. I say wounded learners because as students, we were more focused on having the right answers than on having an inquiring mind and questioning our teachers.

Questions Are the Answer

We believe that asking questions will offend the client. In fact, the opposite is true, as most people feel complemented by our interest and are delighted to answer our questions. There are relatively few (perhaps five percent) who will be offended by questions you ask to determine their corporate needs. *Are you going to drive your business based on the reaction of five percent?* No! The success will come when you manage your business based on 95% of your potential client base. Cater to the masses.

Chapter 8

Problems are like Icebergs—Really!

W HEN SALESPEOPLE HEAR A CUSTOMER IDENTIFY A PROBLEM, their natural instinct is to rise to the occasion with a solution. They don't realize that being so quick to solve a problem shuts down the exploration process. If it's a big problem, there will likely be an assortment of related issues and needs that require exploration and discussion before a solution can be formulated.

Figure 7: Problems are like Icebergs.

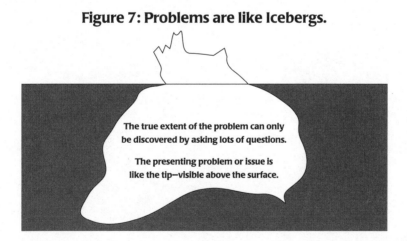

The true extent of the problem can only be discovered by asking lots of questions.

The presenting problem or issue is like the tip—visible above the surface.

It is imperative that the salesperson maintains an open, sincere approach in order to understand the ramifications of the problem. Once again, questioning is the way to learn more. Think of the problem as an iceberg. Less than 20% of it is showing; the remainder is hidden. Failure to uncover the hidden portion of the client's problem presented is like being in a powerboat on a collision course with the iceberg. You will connect with the client, but neither of you will achieve your goal.

Case Study: The Story Behind the Presenting Problem

Recently I accompanied a client, Brad, a commercial real estate salesperson, on one of his sales calls. My role was to observe his actions and audit his sales skills. At a certain point, I was compelled to participate when his client said he definitely needed a parking space for each of his 18 middle to top-level employees. In an attempt to be of service and demonstrate his product knowledge, Brad quickly reassured his client that he could think of three properties with 18 parking stalls. I couldn't resist the opportunity to understand the story behind this problem. I asked the client: *Do you mind telling me why you need those stalls?*

Client: "Well, moving is stressful enough so I don't want any member of the management team to see this as a good time to look for other opportunities. I want to assure them by providing a parking space for them."

Alice: "If you were to lose some team members, how many do you think that would be?"

Client: "About five."

Alice: "What would you estimate to be the cost of hiring and training new replacements and bring them up to speed?"

Client: "At least $200,000 each."

Alice: "Where would these five defectors move to?"

Client: "The competition."

Alice: "How would this impact your reputation in the marketplace and your development of new products?"

Client: "Immensely."

Alice: "Are you aware of other issues which would influence your key employees to move to your competition during the process of relocating?"

Client: "I never thought of that. I've been so preoccupied by the logistics of moving I haven't explored the change with my people."

Alice: "Would it be valuable if we helped you solve this by holding a focus group with your management team? You can help us develop five key questions to pose to your team during a one-hour meeting. The process will be designed so that any prevailing issues will be highlighted."

Other issues were uncovered and the focus group became a critical experience in establishing sufficient trust that Brad (the commercial realtor) was successful in achieving a mandate (exclusive) with his client. As I hope you see from this example, asking questions enabled us to discover the issues behind the problem. One of the key issues was the retention of top-level employees.

In the end, Brad's proposal was able to speak to the real issue—employee retention—where his competitors could not. Brad was successful in beating out his competition and securing a mandate (the one to exclusively search for and negotiate appropriate space). These are excellent results from a few extra questions and another one-hour focus group meeting!

When the ramifications (issues and needs) associated with the major problem are revealed, keep questioning until there are absolutely no more issues to be disclosed. Then, and only then, can you go back and offer solutions. As you offer a solution (or solutions), ask the client to review and comment on the value of the solution to their business. Having the customer state the value of your product or service is the very antithesis of typical "feature" or "benefit" selling. If the salesperson points out the feature and then begins to talk, talk, talk about its benefits, the client may or may not agree. You must check with the client to confirm whether their perception of the features and benefits are aligned with your own.

When you ask your clients about the value of your solution to their problem, they will tell you; and when you write your proposal, the section on value will be familiar to them because they have already shared this information with you. They will have answered all objections and sold themselves. You will be able to refer to issues and concerns about their problems and come to know their expectations of you. Knowing the client agrees with your solution will give you "insider's knowledge." This is truly added value for your client and places you far ahead of the competition.

Self-Centered vs. Other-Centered

Self-centered people tell, explain, and think in the first person:

- *I'm nervous.*
- *Why hasn't he called me?*
- *They're not interested in what I have to say.*
- *She's not nice to me.*

Other-centered people ask questions:

- *I wonder what she's concerned about?*
- *Why is this sales team missing its budget?*
- *How can I help him?*
- *What keeps you awake at night?*

Know that in the beginning, as you practice becoming an other-centered person, you will feel uncomfortable and you will not do it perfectly. *So what?* Keep on using the system, and gradually you will begin to ask other-centered questions naturally. Remember that we are *imperfect human beings*, not *perfect human doings*.

The Consultative Sales Approach

I consult with and train sales teams using a custom development plan for new business. One of the means I've developed to measure results is to design a 2' × 3' chart that plots the number of cold calls made by each member of the team, the number of appointments made, and the number of new clients gained. It's a very colorful, light-hearted, yet highly effective measuring system.

Case Study: The Wrong Way and a Better Way to Sell

When I prepared the chart for printing, I called sales reps from two different printing companies to obtain quotes. The first sales rep began by asking me these questions:

- *How many do you want printed?* (1,500)
- *How many colors?* (4 colors plus varnish)
- *What kind of paper?* (100lb. gloss, coated one side)
- *Any 4-color images?* (No, all line art)
- *Any trimming?* (Trim to 24" × 36")
- *Shipping?* (Bundle in 50s and ship to office)

This rep then said, *"Great. I think that's all I need to know. I'll fax you a quote in the morning."*
"If there's anything else I can do, be sure to give me a call back," she said as she hung up the phone.
That afternoon a sales rep from the second printing company, returned my call and demonstrated an entirely different approach. This person began by creating a comfort zone—in establishing a few ground rules for the call—and then continued with some general questions about my business:

- *How long have you been in business?*
- *How did you happen to go from sales rep to sales consultant, trainer, and speaker?*
- *Is it true that public speaking is the experience to be feared most?*
- *Do you have any competition?*
- *What is your own personal sales process?*
- *Do you still feel disappointed or surprised when you lose a deal?*

He then asked some further, more specific questions about my project:

- *What are you going to use the poster for?*

- *Have you used something similar to this system in the past and if not, why not?*
- *How will using this chart support your connection with a client?*
- *What do you hope to achieve?*
- *How will this help your client?*
- *What if it hangs blankly on the client's wall, with no one recording the information?*
- *Can you contract with the client—in advance—to record the data or remove it from the wall?*
- *What is the possibility of updating this 'wall monitor'?*

Only after Darren had completed asking all these questions did he ask the same sorts of questions about the specifications of the job-as asked by the first printer's sales rep.

The next day I received a quote from both sales reps as promised. The first quote was $1,450; the second, $1,575.

Which printer did I choose? The second printer of course.

If you are confused or in disagreement for my choice of printing service supplier in the foregoing case study, let me explain the basis for my decision.

I am an independent, self-employed businesswoman and every cent counts. However, I ask myself a series of questions in my decision-making process.

How did the sales rep approach me? Was s/he willing to go beyond asking questions about what I wanted? In other words: *Did the rep go through the process of Gently and Tenderly Wounding me with questions? Did s/he show a genuine interest in my project?*

After answering these questions, I was able to make a sound business decision based on the overall picture of the growth of my business, not just the price to print the charts. Consequently, I chose the second sales rep because of the professionalism shown through his concern, curiosity and questioning skills. The difference in price was not a deterrent in using Darren's services because he was able to show a genuine interest in helping me meet my business goals. The importance of this approach is clearly illustrated by this follow-up incident: I was leaving town and wanted the poster printed in time for me to take some of the print run with me and give them to a client. I phoned and explained my need to Darren and he went to the pressroom, packaged 30 posters, and met me at the entrance to the airport parkade.

Figure 8: Problem Investigation.

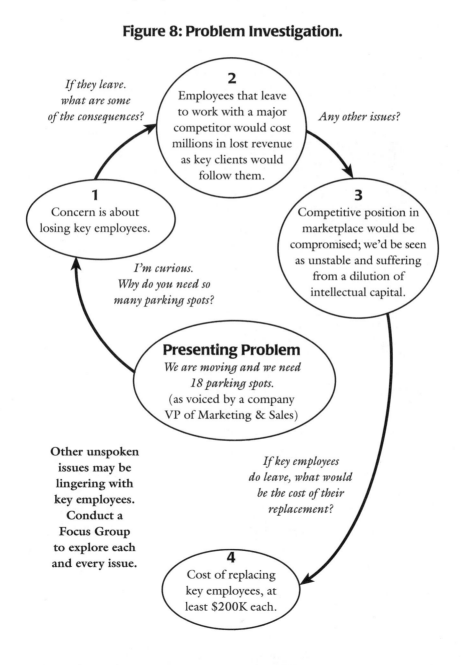

If they leave. what are some of the consequences?

2 Employees that leave to work with a major competitor would cost millions in lost revenue as key clients would follow them.

Any other issues?

1 Concern is about losing key employees.

3 Competitive position in marketplace would be compromised; we'd be seen as unstable and suffering from a dilution of intellectual capital.

I'm curious. Why do you need so many parking spots?

Presenting Problem *We are moving and we need 18 parking spots.* (as voiced by a company VP of Marketing & Sales)

Other unspoken issues may be lingering with key employees. Conduct a Focus Group to explore each and every issue.

If key employees do leave, what would be the cost of their replacement?

4 Cost of replacing key employees, at least $200K each.

Questions That Establish Trust

It is possible, but not probable, that the first printing sales rep would have provided the same service. With his genuine interest in my business and me, Darren showed that he was eminently trustworthy. He was using his personalized version of a *Needs/Issues Assessment* to determine what I wanted and needed. It is important to note that he did not offer solutions until after I answered his questions. His behaviors made me feel at ease as he wrote down my answer to a question and then proceeded to ask me another question. I was quite charmed and felt confident that he could look after the printing of other brochures and literature that, unknown to him, I was redesigning.

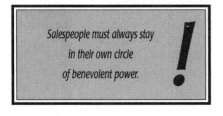

Salespeople must always stay in their own circle of benevolent power.

A manager may have the answers but a good leader has the questions, and Darren was a sales leader when he took charge of that sales call. A customer with power respects and is comforted by salespeople whose power is used for the greater good of the client. Salespeople must always stay in their own circle of benevolent power.

The Pareto Principle

If you offer a solution before you know the pain and consequences resulting from the problem, you will neither find the right solution nor encourage your client to speak freely about their needs and wishes.

Going to a doctor with a raging fever is much the same. Your physician might give you a solution for the fever, but what good is that? The reason for the fever needs to be discovered before it can be treated. To get at the cause, the physician asks questions in order to understand your overall health, not just one symptom.

In selling, the *Pareto Principle* (otherwise known as *the 80/20 Rule*) applies here. You learn about a client's problem by speaking only 20% of the time and listening for the remaining 80%. This means you speak only when asking questions or when responding to a client's questions or comments.

When I began my sales career, I had several experiences that ultimately empowered me. Nevertheless, these experiences were quite difficult to endure at the time because I, like most others, had been socialized not to ask too many questions. Indeed, I believed that to ask questions was to cause others to be offended and have negative feelings toward me.

It wasn't until I listened to a set of tapes by J. Douglas Edwards (my favorite was called *Questions are the Answer*) that I understood the true purpose of asking questions and how clients would feel about those questions. J. Douglas Edwards was among the first to become a published sales trainer. His tapes and books are still available over the internet. Just use his name as the search term. Reading or listening to his works is a good use of your time to discover more of the pearls of wisdom Edwards has to offer.

The Edwards tapes provided me with the initial tools I was lacking in order to succeed as a salesperson. The main learning in these tapes is that Edwards grants us the permission to ask questions and provides us with a simple method of asking. His methodology shows respect for both the customer and the salesperson. I was amazed to discover that prospects actually liked being asked questions. Because I started asking questions, it became clear to them that their concerns and needs were important to me. They appeared to be far more assured that I was not just trying to slide something by them.

It did not take long for me to come to the realization that using questions was the smart way to sell. As my questioning skills improved and I became more comfortable in posing a variety of questions, my sales volumes increased. In the beginning, of course, I felt sheepish and uncomfortable using the questioning process, but I persevered with the techniques, acting with purpose and achieving results. It is important that you do not quit before the miracle happens!

Solicit Objections to Take Control

Soliciting objections is daunting but it allows you to take control of the sales call and to create a comfort zone for the client. If this were easy, there would be much more competition.

Case Study: Why Did You Ask Me That?

My first sales mentor at *Xerox* had been the most successful sales rep in our region for several years in a row. As a new rep, I was lucky to be assigned to work with him.

In the late 70s, the *Xerox 9400* was the largest duplicator manufactured by *Xerox*, and I had already sold one machine that quarter. Since selling another unit would put me on top, ahead of my peers, I was highly motivated to do whatever I could to close that second deal! During a demonstration of this machine the client asked: *How many sheets of paper fit in the auxiliary tray?* I quickly responded: *500 sheets!*

My trainer pulled me aside and said: *You answered too quickly, perhaps just to prove how smart you are. You were doing nothing more than showing off, which is self-centered, not customer-centered! Go back there and ask, 'Why did you want to know how many sheets of paper the auxiliary tray will hold?'*

I felt ashamed, self-conscious, intimidated, and insecure, but I followed his direction anyway. It was with trepidation that I approached the customer and said: *A little while ago you asked how many sheets of paper fit in the auxiliary tray. Why did you ask me that?* The customer's answer led to me selling not just one machine, but two: the 9400 and a smaller model as well.

If I had failed to ask the question I would have missed out on that additional sale, but more importantly, I would not have discovered why the client needed the second machine—so the other employees in the office would not have to line up or wait just to run off a few copies. These results clearly support the notion that questions are the answer. Don't they?

By creating a comfort zone for our prospects, we are deliberately putting ourselves in a zone of discomfort! How paradoxical, yet how appropriate. Our potential profit lies in leaving the comfort zone. No one succeeds by doing the same thing repeatedly. Creating the customer's comfort zone provides us with the ability to speed up the sales process. It allows us to zone in on their real needs, concerns, and objections in a timely fashion. Without the truth—and the truth inherent in the objections these questions uncover—there is only illusion. An illusion, no matter how grand, doesn't pay the bills.

Time is Money

Consider the old adage *time is money*. If you create the call objective and show your professionalism by asking questions you will prove your trustworthiness faster. This will free you up to pursue more opportunities.

Edge Out the Competition

A customer usually finds it easy to identify the main problem. But a salesperson equipped with the ability to ask the customer probing questions will be able to uncover concerns, issues and problems that may have remained hidden. An experienced salesperson will have an arsenal of past customer scenarios and will be able to advise the current client about pitfalls and/or opportunities. If related issues are not uncovered, the solution offered will fall short of the client's needs and the deal will go to the competition.

Chapter 9

Price—The Mother of all Objections

THE PRICE OBJECTION IS A MAJOR OBSTACLE. Everyone feels scrutinized, powerless, and out of control when faced with what I call *the Mother of all Objections*. It's the objection most likely to cause us to scurry back to our offices hoping for rescue.

Our uncomfortable feelings often come from not knowing if our customers are using price as an excuse or trying to play one supplier against the other. *Are we really overpriced for the market?*

Most salespeople are demoralized by the price objection even though selling is a process of learning to live with ambiguity. Salespeople are familiar with most objections and can deal with them. However, prices are set at the corporate office or by someone outside the influence of the salesperson.

When you and your customers draw each other into the sticky, messy discussion of pricing, the focus is not on the value of your product or service. Unfortunately, the focus is on input—the actual product or service itself. However, the focus should be on outcomes—the value, advantages, and benefits—of your product or service. With such a focus, you can explore not only what you hope to achieve, but also what is likely to be achieved.

The Language of Selling

There are three levels of buyers within a corporate structure and you need to know how to talk to buyers at each level. They are *price* buyers, *cost* buyers, and *value* investors, and they each speak a different language. The client's position in the company, or level in the power structure, determines the level of language they use. You must learn to respond to each with the language used at each level. A manager's focus is usually *tactical*, getting the work done right now, while the executive focus is usually *strategic*, visioning towards the future.

89

Frontline managers spend the budget, middle managers allocate the budget to various department supervisors, and the executive level decides on the overall budget for each division. Those who use a frontline purchasing agent's language with the CEO are likely to be shown the door.

Figure 9: Client Orientation to Time Frame and Economic Focus.

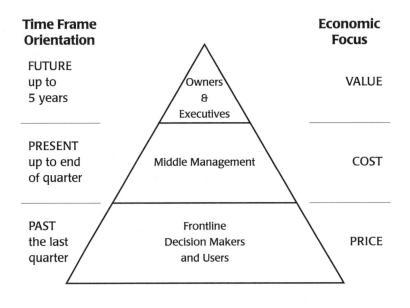

Time Frame Orientation		Economic Focus
FUTURE up to 5 years	Owners & Executives	VALUE
PRESENT up to end of quarter	Middle Management	COST
PAST the last quarter	Frontline Decision Makers and Users	PRICE

Selling to the Front-Line Buyer

Frontline supervisors complete the day-to-day work. Their language and yours must be the same. They will use terms such as: *now, last month, service record, price per item/unit, agenda*, and *budget*. Their economic concern is *price*; their orientation to time is the *past* or *present, short-term*; and they have limited long-range planning responsibility. Their concern is: *What will get the job done today?*

Frontline supervisors are sometimes decision-makers, too. However, it is always with a limited budget, and the time frame is the past. They might reason with themselves, saying: *Last month our expenses were $4,922. I will show my manager how good I am at my job by cutting costs.* Talking about long-term value and asking about strategic plans will intimidate them, and they may judge you as not particularly intelligent.

The questions to ask frontline supervisors are as follows:

- *How can we help you come in under your budget and help you look good for the next quarter too?*
- *How much can you spend without raising the boss's concern?*
- *When we get to the moment of truth, who will make the decision?*

The third question is critically important. It is difficult to ask, but once asked you must sit quietly awaiting an answer. Too many salespeople cave in and begin speaking immediately after asking a question because of the anxiety that silence creates; in so doing they rescue themselves along with the client. Then they may get stuck selling to buyers whose only decision-making power is to say *no*. It is better to wait for the answer and receive one you really would rather not hear, rather than invest time with someone who can explore possibilities but never give you a signed contract.

What recourse do you have if the contact tells you the final decision will be made by a committee? If this were the case, one would hope you have built up enough trust with your contact that you get invited to the committee meeting to make a presentation. If you can't present to the ultimate decision makers, it takes longer to get a contract signed.

Selling to Middle Managers

The next level of selling is to middle managers. The timeline for them is *this quarter* or possibly *the end of this year*. Their economic concern is the overall *cost* of using the product or service. Price is a factor and so are some of the soft dollars, such as increased productivity. The language you hear from this level of client includes terms such as: *department goals, customer service, quality management production, improved mandate, business processes, policy,* and *planning*. These individuals have more responsibility and with that comes a greater expectation of them, by their employer, for higher-level thinking than would be expected of frontline supervisors.

Buyers at the middle level also have an orientation to time which is relatively short-term—the *present* or *immediate future*—so the value you provide must be measured within a few weeks. Here are some questions to ask at this level:

- *How soon do you want to see an increase in production?*
- *What percentage of increase in production are you expecting?*
- *What is the level of desired growth in production?*
- *What can we do right now to improve your bottom line for the next quarter?*
- *Besides yourself, who else will implement your decision?*

These decision-makers have the ability to say yes to some purchases within a specific price range. The danger associated with selling to this level is that once their price range is exceeded you are out of luck, but you may not even know it. That is, you won't know unless you ask: *When you're satisfied that we are a match at an implementation cost of X dollars, will we be able to go ahead on your signature?*

Often middle managers will be able to approve expenditures within certain limits set out by the organization. If the client is unable to approve the expenditure, ask if you can meet with the person who does. Be careful not to sound dismissive when doing this and always approach the client with a non-judgmental tone: *I understand that the price we are discussing is beyond the range for which you can give direct approval. Since we agree that this product/service would benefit your firm, I would like to present this concept at the next meeting of the management team. Will you agree to support me in doing this?*

> The answer is always no if you do not ask!
> If you do ask and the answer is no, regroup and ask again.
> Three attempts to close the sale is not asking too much.
>
> **!**

Does a *no* from middle management mean the death of a potential sale? The answer is not cut and dried. If the client said *no* because of his inability to approve capital expenditures, the sale could still go through at a higher level. On the other hand, if the client is adamant that your product/service is not appropriate for their organization, approaching the next level of management may not be in your best interests. Nevertheless, you must make the effort. The answer is always *no* if you do not ask! If you do ask and the answer is *no*, regroup and ask again. Three attempts to close the sale is not asking too much.

Selling To Executives

The third, executive level in an organization is that of the big-picture visionaries, planners, and strategists. Their timeline is the *future* and their worries are how to stay ahead of the competition, how to be better positioned globally, how to keep abreast of current business practices, and how the organization is performing relative to the company vision and mission. What you sell to them must fit into the larger context, the big picture, or they will not be interested. Their job is to create an organization that generates a steady supply of income while staying ahead of the competition.

The CEO must have something to sell—in effect, the essence of the company—to bankers, brokers, employees, and shareholders. What is it about you or your product that can help her/him do that? The language used with this level of client includes words such as: *strategy, vision, environmental, holistic, core competencies, value proposition, mission,* and *purpose*. Salespeople who address the executive level and use terms like price, competitive, or cheaper will be dismissed without consideration, as if they were speaking gibberish.

Only a small percentage of salespeople have the privilege of presenting their products and services to executive level management—unless the CEO is the only employee of the company. When a company grows to five or more employees or partners, the CEO often becomes sheltered from day-to-day involvement with suppliers and salespeople. Members of an executive management team are often fully booked and their running from one meeting to the next makes it nearly impossible to find an available slot for yet another appointment—especially a sales appointment. Executive team members are also protected by any number of middle management and administrative support staff. Securing a meeting with any member of an executive management team can be difficult—but not impossible. Those adept at handling prospecting objections experience just as much success in calling on executives as they do with prospects at any other level. Salespeople who consistently call on executives are discussed in the first title of my GutsGoalsGlory™ series, *Big Game Hunters and Closers: Attract and Keep Your Super Sellers*.

At the executive level, ask the following questions of yourself as well as the CEO:

- *How does what I sell help these individuals achieve their five-year plan in less time?*
- *Does a reduction in the time allotted to achieve goals automatically equate to a savings in capital?*
- *Do capital expenditures create a heavy debt load in the beginning and only promise relief at the end of the project?*
- *What environmental issues does this company face?*
- *Does the company work in a regulated industry, which might require special considerations to ensure compliance?*
- *What does this company have to do to stay ahead of the competition?*
- *How does this executive stay abreast of the latest trends?*
- *How does this company attract and keep some of the big brains in the industry?*
- *Does my product/service provide a unique answer or solution to a time-consuming or costly activity?*
- *How can the expenditure on products or services be explained to shareholders? What is their value to shareholders?*

Because CEOs are economic buyers, they also respond to these questions:

- *How will this initiative affect the strategic goals of this division?*
- *Has the budget been allocated for this project?*
- *Whose budget will be affected by this purchase?*
- *Whose support will affect the success of this project?*
- *How will my product improve the level of service provided to your clients?*
- *Is there a learning curve for using the product or service that might put us behind on our projected timeline?*

Getting an appointment with a high-level decision maker, but not being able to speak the language, is just as futile as failing to get the appointment. When you know the level of a buyer in a corporation, you need to know their language and their buying power. In all cases, you must be able and prepared to speak the appropriate language.

Avoiding Smokescreens

When salespeople focus on price, they make it difficult for themselves. They condition the client to be a price buyer. When salespeople do not ask questions, they'll never learn about the other issues related to the purchase. If a client objects to the price, it may be a *smokescreen*, but if the sales representative jumps on it, then obviously it worked. In such cases, the executive will negotiate a better price or rid himself of the sales representative.

A price objection may be presented in a variety of formats:

- Your pricing is not competitive.
- I get the most competitive prices now.
- I buy only the cheapest.
- It costs too much.

For salespeople, the natural response is fear. Their tendency is to defend, justify, or placate.

Even worse, the sales rep may promise to match the competitor's price, but must report back to the client to confirm that promise as a lower price must first be authorized by their sales manager. This is the *Hot Potato Approach*—the lowest form of selling—where issues that are too hot to handle are tossed to someone else.

While all clients believe they are price conscious, if clients are not price buyers and you come across as a price seller, they will rapidly lose interest in you. Someone from a large international telephone company cold-called me and asked how much I pay per month for long distance phone service. Here's how that conversation unfolded:

Alice:	*About $350.*
Salesman:	*I can save you over $200 a month.*
Alice:	*But saving money is not my biggest concern.*
Salesman:	*You're telling me that you're not interested in saving $200 a month?*
Alice:	*No, I said that's not my biggest concern.*

My biggest concern is having uninterrupted service for my toll-free number, but he didn't ask. He could have asked: *What is your biggest concern?* Instead, in a voice filled with disdain, he said: *Well, goodbye then!* and hung up.

That salesperson painted himself into a corner by using cost as the only motivation to switch long-distance providers. He could have thought: *Not many people reject a saving of $200. Hmm... What makes her concerns different from the others?* If he had asked, I would have elaborated on my concerns. I may have even switched telephone carriers. I am surprised (and disappointed!) that he did not put a little more effort into that cold call.

Quick Relief For the Price Objection

Imagine yourself saying something like this: *Yes, price is important and I'd like to suggest that we spend time talking price before we decide if we can do business. What I would like to do, if it is okay with you, is to ask you a few questions about other issues that are important to you. Then, when we discuss price, we will already have your needs factored into the equation. That's fair, isn't it?*

If the client says: *Well, just give me a quick price,* you can reply: *I can give you a price now, but it may come in low or high if we don't know all the factors. Either way, we both lose. Before I can quote accurately, I need more information. That's fair, isn't it?*

The Deal Has Come Undone

Sometimes a client will say: *I would have chosen you but your competition had a lower price.* Now what?

Conducting a Competitive Price Analysis

- *Who is your supplier now?*
- *Is your competitor's material/product/service of similar quality and specifications?*
- *Is it fully* (safety) *approved for application?*
- *What is the quantity? Is there a contractual volume guarantee or is it a one-time order?*
- *Can the competitor supply the same volume?*
- *Are terms of payment the same?*
- *For how long is the offer valid?*
- *Is there price stability or a fixed-price period?*
- *Are delivery terms identical?* (FOB origin/destination; freight prepaid/collect, etc.)
- *Is it tank car, tank truck, full truckload, less than truckload price or container specific to your industry?*
- *Is their confidence in and security of supply sourced from domestic producer, import, or warehouse stock?*
- *Is the service package the same?* (technique, delivery, order, lead-time, etc.)
- *Is price gross invoice/net of any rebates/discounts? If rebated, could rebate levels really be achieved?*

If clients cannot, or will not answer these questions, the information may be available from your sales manager or other members of your sales team.

I recommend that you complete a *competitive price analysis*. Actually, give yourself the gift of mental toughness that comes from going through this process on a regular basis. You will become known as a digger, someone not to be trifled with, someone who stays in there till the end.

Strategic Sales

An expert salesperson can combine tactical and strategic selling skills to win far more deals than they lose. The salesperson who does only what needs to be done today is using tactical skills; the salesperson who does what needs to be done to achieve long-term goals is using strategic skills. The salesperson who does both and combines tactical and strategic skills is what I call a *converger*—and typically outperforms the pack.

Strategic salespeople must be fluent in all three languages of selling. When they hear a language, they must be able to respond in kind. They have learned to test the field by using particular phrases and expressions. If a conversation can be built around those phrases, the prospect and sales professional are speaking the same language and the result is usually good for business. It is incumbent upon sales professionals to learn the language spoken at all levels of their industry.

Just Another Form of Feedback

The price objection, like other objections, can be dismantled and used to improve your chances of success. That means speaking the right language to the client and embracing all issues or concerns regarding price-the *Mother of All Objections*. If you can view price objections as just another form of feedback to be explored, you will stand out from the crowd and demonstrate your professionalism by transforming the objection and turning it to their advantage. Salespeople must learn to dance with objections and turn them into *the juice of the sale*.

Salespeople must learn to dance with objections and turn them into the juice of the sale.

Chapter 10

Warm Up the Cold Call

Y OU WILL RECALL, FROM CHAPTER ONE, that there are two main reasons why prospects raise objections. If you do not remember why, and you wish to go back to the beginning of the book to review those reasons, don't! Because a fear of objections is the most significant reason why salespeople avoid making cold calls, the reasons bare repeating here. First, objections work to get rid of incompetent salespeople, and second, they help separate good salespeople from the rest of the pack who do not know objections are worth their weight in gold—and are the juice of the sale!

Each time you receive, acknowledge, and deal with an objection during the prospecting call, your chances of getting the appointment will increase by about 25%. If you were to ask for an appointment three times and you successfully dealt with any and all objections on each occasion, you would have raised your chances of getting an appointment to 75%. Occasionally, a prospect will become annoyed with this sort of persistence. Do not let the reaction of five percent of your contacts influence the way you approach the other 95%.

Not backing down demonstrates a belief in yourself and in your product or service. You are seen as a leader, a person who respects the burning desire to succeed. Those who can manage their uncomfortable emotions well enough to ask again and again for a desired outcome demonstrate personal power. Some readers may be asking: *Won't the client get angry if I continue to ask them for an appointment?* The answer to this question is going to vary with every potential client. If you carefully integrate the request for a meeting with a clear respect for client concerns, you are not likely to cause offence.

Each time you deal with a concern and suggest the benefits of a meeting, your chances of obtaining the appointment improve. Remember, the client wants to be treated with respect and if you acknowledge the value of their time and money, ultimately you will be rewarded.

People with power are comforted by displays of power. If you are seen as being reticent, your "power clients" will presume you're likely to waste their time. They have their own power so they don't need anyone to be submissive to them. If you are unable to handle a few objections, you will remain a lower-level decision maker. If you do not display appropriate power, that is where you belong. This may sound harsh, but it is true. You must see yourself as the equal—a peer—of your client. You have something of value to offer them and they have a problem that you can solve for them. It's an ideal match!

Telephone Objections: The Kiss of Death

Telephone objections can be the *Kiss of Death* because if you can't get an appointment you can't engage in the selling process wherein you provide a solution to your client and their company—a solution that will help them, in turn, provide a solution to their own customers. I call telephone objections the *Kiss of Death* because even seasoned salespeople back away from such encounters. If you back away, you lose the opportunity to develop a connection with the client.

The following six telephone objections are those which I have encountered most frequently and their generic nature means they are not sales industry sector-specific and can apply to virtually any product or service you are selling. All salespeople have encountered them at one time or another, and they have beaten many of us. With practice, all of these objections can be stickhandled successfully and dealt with in a professional manner.

The six *Kiss of Death* telephone objections are:

1. Can I tell him who is calling?
2. Can I tell her exactly what this is about?
3. Can you send a brochure?
4. I'm very busy; I don't have time.
5. Can you call me back?
6. Will you confirm with me the day before?

When next you encounter any of these objections consider incorporating the following ideas into your own responses.

1. Can I tell him/her who's calling?

This response is rarely heard these days because of voice mail. However, it's still possible to reach a gatekeeper whose job it is to screen salespeople from taking up the boss's time. The trick is to prevent the person from asking you that question. If you begin your request by giving your name, you have answered the question before it is asked.

Begin each prospecting call with: *Hello, my name is _____ and I'm calling for Ron Hughes. Is he there please? I'll hold.* Then do not utter one sound until after the receptionist speaks. Remember, the receptionist is conditioned to ask: *Can I tell him who's calling?* When you pre-empt the usual response and break the receptionist's stride, your chances of having him or her follow your suggestion is much greater, but only if you stay silent. Asking a question and then holding onto silence is one way you can stand in your own circle of power.

In our society, we seem to have a low tolerance for silence. More than six or seven seconds causes most people to feel anxious. Along with the receptionist, you will also feel anxious, but because you're the one causing the anxiety you should be able to tolerate it. Salespeople with too much empathy will want to rescue the receptionist. Salespeople who are willing to break the silence are actually rescuing themselves, not the client. Their discomfort rises to an intolerable level and they rescue themselves and the receptionist by speaking. The empathy you feel for the receptionist may be real, but resist the urge to speak. Let the tension build. Don't speak. The receptionist will not be able to tolerate the silence, and the quickest way to handle it is to give you what you want.

The silence you create is cold so you must precede it by speaking slowly. Your voice must be friendly, clear, concise, and warm. The mixture is highly effective for getting what you want—an appointment and the opportunity to provide value to this company via your product or service. If you don't call, how will the company know about you?

When you are put through to your contact you may have to settle for voice mail. Whether or not the voice mail message asks you to contact a specific person, press zero. This will increase your chances of reaching someone who can share some insight into the comings and goings of your contact.

A great way to gain the assistant's help and commitment is by using nine magic words. Use them whenever you need help and they are: *I have a problem, and I need your help.* Then pause to let the words sink in. The response will usually be warm and helpful. By admitting you are human and need help, you have placed the listener in a position of power. I call this an act of *courageous vulnerability.*

2. Can I tell her exactly what this is about?

When you respond to this objection, and any other objection, you disarm the receptionist by agreeing with her. You answer quite correctly and quickly that, of course, you can tell her. However, you are not going to, not exactly, although you are going to give her the answer she wants to hear. This is called receiving the objection. Remember the story about the bully with the stick in the introduction?

Notice that your response must begin by receiving the objection. The purpose of this is to present yourself as non-threatening. When you appear to agree with the request, defenses are lowered and receptivity is easier to establish.

Yes, of course you can tell her. It's about a change in corporate policy and I need to speak with her about that today. Is she in please? I'll hold.

Again, be silent after you have stated your request. It is doubtful that any frontline person will want to quibble with "a change in corporate policy." Besides, what did you actually say? Nothing yet...but whatever you are offering could result in a corporate change in policy, couldn't it?

The second benefit of using bafflegab, or non-specific words designed to impress, is that many receptionists won't remember what you said after your call has been transferred to the manager. The phrase "a change in corporate policy" is not typical of the vocabulary of most receptionists.

☎ 3. Can you send me a brochure?

Salespeople rarely identify this request for what it really is—an attempt to dodge any further communication. It is a polite way for the prospect to say *no!* and still be able to think of himself as a nice person. Remember, we all have some degree of difficulty with saying *no*—and that's no less true for our prospects! Because of the average salesperson's naivete, this objection frequently works. Many salespeople say: *Of course I can.* They get the address but often don't follow up and, if they do, the prospect or their assistant will usually toss the brochure. The average salesperson also considers this to have been a successful transaction because they were able to maintain their *Happy Ears Syndrome*—they were let down nicely. They did not get the order but are relieved that their sensibilities are intact. What a waste! Better to get the appointment or the order and repair one's disrupted sensibilities later. The following alternative response will help you stay in the driver's seat:

Yes, of course I can send you a brochure, but would it establish a win-win relationship? Pause for a few seconds after you ask this question, then follow with another: *As nice as my brochure is, it couldn't possibly establish a win-win relationship. If it's all right with you, I'd like to set a time to meet with you... so you'll get a sense for me and I'll get a sense for you. Then you can decide if we should have a longer meeting or not. Does that sound fair to you?*

By handling the objection in this way, you demonstrate how you are different from the others. Notice that you receive the objection by agreeing that you can send a brochure. However, you also negotiate for an appointment.

Sometimes the "send me a brochure" objection involves a contact from out of town. You know that traveling to see this contact is an unwise use of your time at this stage of the relationship, so sending a brochure might be a "toe in the door." If you agree to send a brochure, also try to obtain a commitment from the prospect with a preliminary contract. Here's how it works:

Of course I can send you a brochure, but let me ask you a tough question (do not pause)... *How long do you think it will take to reach you if I send it today—10 days or so?* (wait for an answer) ...Great, and then you need a chance to look through it. ...*Great, so what I'll do, if it's all right with you, is call two weeks from today so I can ask you some questions and let you know how we work. That's fair, isn't it?*

By setting up a time to have a telephone conversation after sending the brochure, you've created an agreement to reconnect as if you were meeting in the same town. Instead of a face-to-face meeting, at least you have a phone appointment.

4. I'm very busy, I don't have time.

This objection is not intended to show how important the client is. It's used because it rolls off the tongue easily, and because it's an effective way to get rid of salespeople. To overcome this objection, as with the receptionist, you must provide something different to break the pattern.

Oh, I didn't mean this week, or even the next. I was thinking of three or four weeks from now, so why don't we pencil something in for the last Thursday of the month? Would morning or afternoon be better for you? It's a wide open field for me that day so why don't you choose? Again, be silent after you have made this request and suggestion.

What does it mean when you say pencil something in? It signifies flexibility, not cornered options, which is a way of providing a measure of psychological comfort. You're showing your empathic side. Once the prospect has chosen morning or afternoon, you assert your goals by saying: *Can we make this a win-win arrangement?* (Do not pause here; it only appears that you are asking for an answer.) *That is, if something comes up for you, you give me a call to reschedule, and I'll do the same for you. That's fair, isn't it?* Once the client agrees to contact you in case of a change, be sure to provide your cell, pager, and office numbers.

Note: It's not your job to manage your prospect's timetable. For more information on this, see the final kiss of death telephone objection: *Will you confirm with me the day before?*

Psychological Tie-Downs

You may have noticed that at the end of each request, I add: *That's fair, isn't it?* This is called a *psychological tie-down*. That is, you ask a question that stimulates the prospect's psychological need to say *yes* by tapping into their own enlightened self-interest to maintain their own image of being a fair person.

Two questions to which people always answer *yes* are:

1. *Do you have a sense of humor?*
2. *Are you a fair person?*

If you end your requests with, *That's fair isn't it?* or *Does this seem fair to you?* you tap into their psychological need to see themselves as fair.

If you want to validate this claim, you can develop a set of questions, including the two mentioned above, to which people can give only a *yes* or *no* answer. Test your friends, co-workers or even strangers on a street corner, and experience the results for yourself. It would be a shame if you didn't utilize this knowledge for the good of your business success.

5. Can you call me back?

It is true, sometimes you catch a person at a busy time. When I make a prospecting call, I never ask if it's a good time to call because it's too easy for a prospect, recognizing it as a prospecting call, to say: *Sorry, I'm busy.* If prospects are truly busy, it's up to them to say so. If I make a call and receive this objection, I respond with: *Of course, I can call you back. When would you like me to call?* Again, be silent after you asked this question.

If you call back a second time and they ask you to call back again then you engage in conversation this way:

Mr./Ms. Customer, can I ask you a tough question? I'm going to feel uncomfortable asking it, and maybe you will feel uncomfortable answering it. Sometimes people don't say no because they don't want to hurt my feelings. But it's okay by me if you say no.

If they do say *no*, respond with: *Thank you for being so candid. I appreciate your respecting my time and yours.* And move on!

6. Will you confirm with me the day before?

This is my favorite objection. I know customers say this because they want to be regarded as nice, reasonable people. They think to themselves: *I may have said yes to the poor salesperson, but I'll just avoid her by being busy when she calls back later.* This is passive-aggressive behavior intended to try to throw you off, so don't fall for it.

> There is no honor in having a prospect waste your time. You must see yourself as equal to your customer. **!**

Establish equality and peerage by saying: *Of course I can confirm with you the day before, but will you agree to a win-win arrangement between us? That is, if anything comes up for me, I'll be sure to call you* [pause] *and you do the same for me* [no pause]. *That sounds fair, doesn't it?*

To improve the chances of the client calling you, should a timetabling conflict arise, you might wish to provide more than one means of contact—for example, your office phone number and a pager or cellular. This would make it difficult for a client to use the excuse that they were unable to reach you. You can eliminate that excuse by providing options for contacting you.

In these six *Kiss of Death* scenarios, you must operate in the circle of your own benevolent power in a polite fashion. There is no honor in having a prospect waste your time. You must see yourself as equal to your customer. Yes, there is a risk that you will show up and the prospect will not be there. It is far riskier to call prospects to confirm the meeting because it gives them the opportunity to reconsider your value to them. When they ask you to confirm the day before, they are asking you to be responsible for their time management. That is what assistants do, not professional salespeople who are their peers.

Embrace the Objection

Objections are just another way prospects have for stalling the sales call process. When you learn to embrace the objection, to clarify its meaning for the client, your opportunity to close the sale will be greatly enhanced.

Each sector of the sales industry has unique objections. Examples of generic sales industry objections are listed in the Chapter 12. As you read them, you'll notice the answer to one objection may be similar to the answer offered for an objection in another sector of the industry. Despite apparent repetition, I believe you will be well served if you persevere and read every example, even though they may not deal with your specific sector of the industry. Chances are you will begin to pick up on ideas or themes which you have not previously considered which you can adapt or modify, tailoring them to your own industry sector and particular sales interests and responsibilities.

Chapter 11

Break Out of Voice Mail Jail

TECHNOLOGY IS GREAT AS FAR AS IT GOES, but from a salesperson's point of view sometimes it goes too far. Technology becomes a barrier to sales success when the people we are wanting to reach hide behind the gadgetry: call display, message centers, e-mail systems, and voice mail.

Some veteran sales professionals yearn for the days of old when a receptionist intercepted calls. At least then, they could approach the receptionist with logic, reason, force, or just plain charm.

Voice mail is impossible to charm or influence. However, there are several methods to decrease its negative impact on your career. The most vital step is to clean up your own voice mail response. Does your voice mail say the obvious? Either of these voice mail statements—*I can't come to the phone right now or I'm either on the phone or away from my desk*—are rhetorical. In both cases, you are stating the obvious and giving information that sounds like it was borrowed from the cliche crowd.

Do you have a commitment of response time on your voice mail? My voice mail states: *I'll call you back as soon as I can, I promise, and my personal goal is to do that within four hours.* When you are unimpeachable about your voice mail manners, you can begin to expect others to respond to you in the same way.

Next, have a long list of names that you consider prospects. If at any time you have only four or five names to call, it's easy to give up and assume that everyone has voice mail these days so there's no point in calling. As part of your sales arsenal, a list of at least 25 prospects to call is a blessing. If you haven't compiled a list of at least 25 prospects, do so right now. Then vary the time you call. Some people get to their office early before 8 am, or stay late after 5 pm. Some people answer their phone during their lunch hour and still others answer their phone whenever it rings. You just never know, and you will never know unless you attempt the call.

Oddly enough, one of the best times to prospect and have the phone answered personally is Friday afternoons. This may be because meetings are usually not scheduled at this time, or because the weekend is around the corner and people are more relaxed, and they bend their own rules around answering telephone calls. Whatever the reason, give Friday afternoons a try!

> When you are unimpeachable about your voice mail manners, you can begin to expect others to respond to you in the same way.

It bears repeating that the first step is developing a great prospect list. Add to that the determination to connect. When you establish an intention to connect and then focus on that goal, success is more likely. Focus and intention is a powerful combination. It's as if the force of your will causes you to be more creative and more alert to possibilities than if you have a defeated *voice mail jail* attitude. Focus is everything.

Another technique callers can use is to press *67 before making the call. This blocks your name and number from being displayed on a phone set with call display. I use this function only if I have to call a prospect more than once—and only after I have previously left a message.

To Leave or Not To Leave a Message

One question that begs to be answered is: *should I leave a voice mail message?* My opinion: don't leave more than one and, if you don't get a call back within 24 hours, don't leave another. Leaving more than one message can make potential clients even less willing to meet with you. It's important to keep phoning, though, varying the time of day and perhaps dialing *67 beforehand.

If you're prospecting and have a long list of people to call, leave a voice mail at your own discretion. If you do leave a message, leave no more than one. People feel guilty for not keeping a commitment to return all their voice mail messages (as per their recorded message) and feel annoyed when nagged; you don't want either of those emotions—guilt or annoyance—associated with you.

Oftentimes, you can also "zero out," that is, press "0" for further options. If you reach a real, live human being, you have a golden opportunity to ask questions about your prospect's schedule. If an assistant, receptionist, or secretary answers, remember to use the nine magic words: *I have a problem and I need your help.* Then pause to let those words sink in. The response will usually be warm and helpful because you've admitted that you're human, and you have put the assistant, receptionist, or secretary in a position of power. You'll probably get answers to your questions.

When you do leave a message, begin with your name and phone number, and be sure to say the number slowly. Imagine that you are the conductor of an orchestra using a baton to draw the number in the air. Speak clearly and slowly, and then deliver a short, pithy message. At the end of your message, leave your name and phone number again. This will make it more convenient for a listener who may be retrieving messages from the car or the office. Nobody wants to replay the whole message just to note your name and number. Always do what you can to make it easy for your prospects to return your calls.

River of No Returns

I wish I knew why people don't return telephone calls. I am amazed by the frequency with which I encounter people who record an outgoing message that closes with: *...and I'll get back to you as soon as I can-*and then they don't call back! We could presume they're so disorganized that they are incapable of returning a call. Yes, maybe they have to return 20 calls a day, but that's life if you're in business and you have a telephone.

Of course, the people for whom you leave voice mail messages may experience the same problem—they don't get their calls returned. If your intention is to return phone calls selectively, compose your outgoing message accordingly. Even a statement as ordinary *as I'll return your call as soon as I can* sounds like a promise. Be as good as your word. Your message can leave an impression on the caller. Why not just return the call?

One very successful mortgage manager I know carries two cell phones with him—even when he's on the golf course with his best customer. He respects the power of returning all his calls. In today's business world, it pays to understand that information rules. What if someone received ten calls but only one contained that golden opportunity? It's probable that millions and millions of dollars worth of opportunities are missed because people don't return calls. Sages and mystics tell us that we eventually get back what we put out. If that's the case, there's an abundance of poor telephone and voice mail etiquette building up bad karma—and losses will be forthcoming for those who don't bother to return their calls.

What if someone phones you, leaves a message for you to call and when you do, they don't call you back? The frustration could be minimized if each of you left a message asking specific questions or giving more precise directions. I have used this process to solve an issue in a timely manner that otherwise would have taken up much more time. Used in this manner, voice mail becomes your friend.

Participating in telephone tag when real communication is occurring is not nearly as frustrating as waiting for a return phone call. If you don't receive the promised call, you may have to rely on your sense of humor to stay positive.

Colin, a very busy vice-president of a national commercial real estate company, called to ask about an issue relating to sales consulting for his team. With due diligence I returned his call within my committed time frame, but received no response. My second (remember he initiated the call to me) message went like this: *Colin, I remember my first date; I remember my first kiss; I remember my first boyfriend and I remember my first heartbreak. It occurred when that boyfriend said he'd return my call and he never did! Soooo, please don't break my heart again.* Colin received that message after a long day of grueling negotiations and it made him laugh out loud. He gladly returned the call.

Incremental Contracting Communication Process

It is true that we suffer disappointment and resentment only if we have unmet expectations. To manage this, create an incremental contract with your client about the best way to stay in contact. An incremental contract is a series of small steps you negotiate with the prospect, made as the sales process evolves and moves towards a formal agreement to do business. I always try to implement the process but, when I forget or wimp out, it results in feelings of regret.

Here's an example of incremental contracting:

Alice: *Connie, do you agree we are a team—working together on this project—and we'll need to touch base from time to time?*

Connie: *Of course.*

Alice: *As part of my professional practice, I return my calls within four hours. However, everyone is different. What would be a reasonable time for you to get back to me if I leave a voice mail message?*

Connie may tell me that voice mail is less convenient for her and touching base via e-mail would be preferable. If so, we should come to an agreement on e-mail response times.

Incremental contracting with a client is part of advanced sales communication. Novice communicators may feel uncomfortable with the process and step back from the challenge, instead choosing to endure the frustration of waiting and wondering. Salespeople who choose incremental contracting will stand out as leaders—willing to do whatever it takes to succeed.

Elegant Objection Handling

A laudable goal is to be *spiritually elegant*, acting and speaking with equanimity and grace. If I don't intend to return calls in my voice mail, I would say so in my phone message. If you say you will return calls, then do so, even at great inconvenience. It's more than a matter of common courtesy—you never know when prosperity will show up via a voice-mail message.

Chapter 12

Generic Sales Industry Objections

ANYONE WHO HAS EVER WORKED IN SALES has almost certainly been on the receiving end of objections concerning their services or products made by their prospects or potential clients. What's also true is that not all salespeople know how best to handle those objections successfully—in the moment. Before each of my sales training sessions, I invite participants to compile a list of difficult objections they have encountered to which they wish they'd had made a more successful or appropriate response. I also ask participants to compile a second list of problem sales situations which have caused them stress, anxiety or conflict and which they feel interfered with or undermined the sales potential of the meeting. The objections and situations presented in the following two chapters have been selected from among the many examples submitted during these training sessions.

Many of the objections and situations submitted by participants attending my sales training sessions are generic in nature and not specific to any particular sector of the sales industry. Those objections and situations reported with the greatest frequency were selected for inclusion in this book. As you review these examples, I hope you will learn to reframe and accept objections and problem situations as simply being part of life on life's terms for every salesperson. No one is exempt. Objections and problem situations are just *speed bumps* on the road to sales success.

As part of my professional practice, I am available for consulting and individual coaching on handling objections and problem sales situations which are specific to your own sales industry sector. Contact me by E-mail at: **salesobjections@alicewheaton.com**.

Practical Solutions to Common Objections

Objection: *We have a preferred supplier we're happy with.* (Just because prospects say this doesn't mean it is true!)

Solution: *Yes, of course you do. Let me ask you a question:* (don't pause, as this is a hook to create interest in the question that follows). *As a business leader how many business or professional magazines do you read each month?* If there is no quick response, continue with: *Could it be as many as four or five? Would you agree that it's important to be open to new ideas and solutions? If you are willing to invest some time with me, I guarantee the new insights and information you will gain will have been worth your time.*

Objection: *The person you need to speak to is in a meeting. Leave your phone number and I'll have him call you back.*

Solution: *It sounds as if your boss is very busy.* A typical response will be: *Yes, she's very busy.* You now identify with the assistant's concern by saying: *No, no, I don't want to burden her by adding another phone message. When do you expect her to be back in her office? Does she answer her own phone? I wonder if you can tell me the best time to call her?*

Objection: *Your turnaround time is too long.*

Context: The salesperson's instinct is to react to the objection as if it were in need of being solved immediately. Instead, be curious. Get the story behind the statement, as discussed in Chapter 7. Try and uncover this information by asking more questions. Embrace the objection before you stickhandle it.

Solution: *Tell me more about that...*
What is the ideal turnaround?
Why is that?
What are the consequences for you if turnaround is too long?
How are you affected?
Who else is affected? How so?

Objection: *Your competition says that your solution is overkill.*

Solution: *Let me ask you a question. Would you ever put yourself in the vulnerable position of having me advise you about their product? I'm not an expert on their product; and they are not experts on mine.*

Objection: *We're still thinking about it.*

Context: If clients need to spend long periods to think over their decision, they may need to go through a due-diligence process. You need to go back and complete a *Needs/Issues Assessment* and review their key motivators. In the sales call process, this is called requalifying. If they say: *I'll think about it*, without allowing you to revisit the issues, what they really mean is *no*! Just move on!

Objection: *I've dealt with you before and I wasn't happy with you then.*

Solution: *It is my understanding that you didn't feel our services were at the level you expected. That's why I suggest we visit. Wouldn't you agree that it is impossible, in your business and in mine, to provide a perfect product or service 100% of the time, although we do strive to meet those standards? When we miss the mark we like to know, so we use it as an opportunity to become even* *better. Is that true for your company?* If the response here is *yes,* then continue: *That's what we do, too, and I'd like to talk to you about our changes and improvements to see if they fit with your needs now. That's fair, isn't it?*

Objection: *I deal directly with a supplier and I'll have to pay more to deal with you.*

Solution: *Of course you want to receive value for your money and certainly you'd want to stay with your lower-priced, current supplier—so long as they are supporting your assets the way they ought to be supported. What I'd suggest is that we set a time to compare the value received from each company.*

Objection: *We are committed to another supplier/line of product right now and we don't want to change.*

Solution: *Oh, I'm not suggesting you switch all your business to me. Wouldn't you agree that with today's client being much more discriminating, it's important to know about other options and possibilities? That's what I'd like to discuss with you. After we meet you may still decide not to change, but you will have more information upon which to base your decision.*

Objection: *I'm selling the business.*

Solution: *Interesting...could you tell me a little about the process of finding a buyer and being willing to part with your own creation?* The answer may shed some light on issues, which only you can solve!

Objection: *I need to discuss this with my partner/s.*

Context: You need to have contact with both/all partners. If this hasn't happened, here is a plausible solution.

Solution: *Of course you need to speak to your partner/s. You know, it's taken me many years to accumulate the experience as well as continuing education to maintain an expertise in this product line. When you visit with your partners, they will likely ask questions that you can't answer—which may be frustrating for you. What I'd suggest is we set up an appointment for all of us. Now, where and when can I meet with all of you?*

Option: If the client responds that meetings are nearly impossible to arrange due to the varied schedules of all the partner/s, then suggest arranging a telephone conference call to discuss the products and services you are selling.

Objection: *I know I said I would go over all the materials you gave me in the initial presentation, but I haven't had time.*

Solution: *That's why I called. It occurred to me that you're busy and might not have the time. What I'd like to do is spend a few minutes with you going over some of the key points again, because that will save you time in the long run.*

Objection: *Are your prices better than ABC Company?*

Solution: *Price is a very important issue and one that needs a great deal of discussion. What I'd like to do, if it's all right with you, is to look at all the related issues and items you require from me. When we're clear on those, then we can spend as much time as you need discussing price. Does this sound fair to you?*

(Also refer to Chapter 9: *Price—The Mother of all Objections.*)

Objection: *Your prices are too high.*

Context: If they refer to added value, use it to move directly into the process for establishing your product's value.

Solution: *Let me ask you a question. Do your sales representatives ever hear the same concern when they are presenting your own company's products or services?* (The buyer will probably say yes.) *Exactly! Why would your prospects say that about you? How do you help them understand your company's price position?*

Objection: *We don't have a budget for your product.*

Solution: *Oh, the budget! Do you notice how often you need to be creative with your accounting and move resources around? What I'd like to do, if it's all right with you, is work with you to achieve your budget goals, streamline the buying processes, and create the best product mix to fit your budget. If your purchases have been made for this year, we could begin to plan for next year's budget.*

Objection: *Is that your best rate?*

Solution: *Best rates are important, and I'd like to spend as much time as necessary in going over how we derive our rates and offer them to you. In addition, it's important that we understand what else is critical for you in our provision of service and pricing. Therefore, what I'd like to do, if it's okay with you, is meet and learn what would be of value to you. I can provide you with an outline of how we work, which you can evaluate for yourself. If you feel that our companies are a good* *match, lets make an appointment to meet again. Does that approach sound fair to you?*

Objection: *How can I verify the quality of your product?*

Solution: *Let me ask you a question* (don't wait for approval): *What would it take for you to be confident about our product? If you were confident about the quality of our product, would you be willing to go ahead?*

Objection: *We've tried your company in the past and were not happy.*

Solution: *That's why I'm calling! As you know, in business* (pause here because you don't want to sound as if you are defending or justifying the past, which can't be done anyway) *decisions are made using the best policies available at the time, both in your company and mine, wouldn't you agree? Therefore, what I'd like to do, if it's all right with you, is set a time to meet with you so you can tell me how your business has changed in the interim, and I can tell you how we've changed. Then you can tell me if we can go forward from there. Does that sound fair to you?*

Objection: *We don't require your service/product right now.*

Solution: *Well, that's why I'd like to see you; I believe in being proactive. I would like to meet with you before you ever use our services and/or products so you will know in advance if our companies are a match and could work well together. Isn't that proactive?* (Client will likely agree). *Exactly! So what I'd suggest is that we meet for a short time so we get a sense for each other and you can tell me if we should talk about doing business or not.*

Objection: *I'm not interested.*

Solution: *Oh, I wouldn't want to see me either if I had no value*
              to bring to your company, and that's why I'm calling.
              Ten other purchasers (name them) like you found our
              approach to business to be very supportive for them to
              get their job done with less worry, added convenience,
              and great products. Why don't we meet? You tell me
              what works and doesn't work for you, and I'll tell you
              how other clients have found the system helps their
              business. Then you tell me what you think. Does that
              sound fair to you?

The Engaged Customer

Customer objections should be seen as a glad moment for the salesperson, because at this point the prospect/client is engaging you. A prospect or customer who does not provide any feedback is disengaged and inaccessible.

Learning to receive and respond to objections is the first step in achieving success.

Chapter 13

Problem Situations that Threaten the Sale

I T IS NOT NECESSARILY THE INABILITY OF THE SALESPERSON to handle objections that stalls the selling process. There are problem sales situations which can be even more challenging than any given objection. The problem sales situations presented in this chapter were selected from among the responses received from participants in my sales training seminars. They represent the most frequently occurring situations which sales professionals reported have caused them most stress, anxiety or conflict and which they feel interfered with or undermined the sales potential of a meeting.

Practical Solutions to Problem Situations

Situation: *I'm being totally ignored by a prospect, even though I am dealing with him the same way as I've dealt successfully with others.*

Context: All prospects are not the same! Being ignored can lead you to feel rejected, but your questioning skills will help you discover the *why* behind the prospect's behavior.

Solution: Ask the prospect the following three questions:

1. *What one thing do you wish your current supplier would keep doing?*

2. *What one thing do you wish your current supplier would stop doing?*

3.   *What one thing do you wish your current supplier would start doing?*

Solution: *Voila!* The answers to these questions will provide the information you need to proceed.

Situation: *During a cold call with a business owner, there are many interruptions and we're short of time. I find myself doing all the talking and feel that our relationship is not developing.*

Solution: Don't fall into the trap of talking more than your prospect/client. You need to learn how to question. Talking, telling, or explaining is so disrespectful. No wonder a relationship isn't developing. Review Chapter 6: *Questions Are the Answer, Aren't They?*

Situation: *I find it hard to be taken seriously because I am a female and 23 years old. Some men will not acknowledge that I'm even in the room.*

Solution: Don't act prissy. Soccer players play by soccer rules. Baseball players play by baseball rules. It's important for women to understand and practice the rules of business, which includes how to dress. The following suggested reading will help with fast-forwarding your understanding of these rules. Claim your share, but don't begin to blame men for your lack of success. You wouldn't credit men, or anyone else, for your achievements. Thinking: *it's because I am a woman*, makes you a victim. *Why not use your energy to figure a way around or through those gender barriers instead of fighting imaginary battles?*

You will find further help in the following books:

Harragan, B. (1977). *Games mother never taught you: Corporate gamesmanship for women.* New York, NY: Warner Books.

Malloy, T.J. (1996). *Dress for success for women.* New York, NY: Warner Books.

Rubin, H. (1997). *The princess Machiavelli for women.* New York, NY: Dell Publishing.

(The first two titles may be out of print. However, they should be available at your local library.)

I remember reading a story about a very wealthy man who gave Marilyn Monroe a pair of large emerald and diamond earrings. As she entered a room people would exclaim: *What beautiful earrings!* She stopped wearing them, so intent was she on having nothing, not even earrings, distract from the image of her as a professional. When saleswomen dress in a manner that draws attention to themselves instead of their business, their credibility is affected. *Why become 'eye candy' before people have a chance to be impressed by your intellect or ability as someone who can solve a serious business problem for them?*

Situation: *Clients don't phone back when they say they will.*

Solution: *Did you think they really would?* They said they would just to let you down gently, and to maintain their self-image of being a nice person. When they tell you this, respond with something like: *I wouldn't think of burdening your day. I make lots of calls in the course of a day so I'd like to be responsible for contacting you. Would this Friday afternoon work for you?*

Situation: *At times, it feels like the customer is not listening to what I'm saying.*

Solution: Nor should they! The most attention you can reasonably expect from anyone is 45 seconds at a time—unless you're talking about his or her needs, issues, concerns, life, etc. Remember the *80/20 Rule*. Let the customer have 80% of the airtime and restrict yourself to the remaining 20% and even then, you should try and limit your dialogue to asking questions for greater clarification. Questions are the answer because they uncover more information.

Situation: *We've passed your information on to the line manager, and he hasn't called back yet.* How do I get past this when the company insists I go through HR?

Solution: Get the name of the line manager and act as if you haven't already sent a package. Make a cold call, set the appointment, nurture the process, and do the deal.

Situation: *A client was very rude even though I did my best to appease him and follow up on information he was asking for. Later he laid a complaint, saying I was incompetent.*

Answer: I don't cater to rude clients or endure rude people. They are behaving out of a place of fear and are, in fact, asking for recognition in the best way they know how. While I don't cater to them, I do not counterattack. I try to be gracious and clear, and my response might be: *I sense that you and I are not a match.* Consider relinquishing the account so your sales manager can reassign the client to another member of your team. There is no shame in withdrawing from what looks to be a no-win situation.

Situation: *My business clients need to get approval from their other advisors, such as legal counsel and accountants. Sometimes the advisors reject the proposal just because they were not the one's who suggested it.*

Solution: This sounds like a judgment you're making. *How do you know it was just because...?* Become clear on the decision-making process, and who the final arbiters are, before you make the proposal. Sell to those who ultimately make the decision/s.

Situation: *How do I deal with a customer who automatically treats me like the enemy for no apparent reason?*

Solution A: I don't deal with such people, let alone customers. However, you might openly and candidly create a context in which to ask the client about this: *Mr. _____, can I ask you a question that might be difficult for you to hear?* (They will always say yes to this.) *My sense is that you have some strong opinions about my company or me. Can you tell me about that?*

Solution B: Another approach for this situation is to question the client in a softer tone by asking: *Would you be able or willing to share your experiences with me? It's important to me that I understand why you are cautious about meeting with me.* Most clients will readily talk about past problems; however, it is important that you recognize and accept a *no* if the person is unwilling to share their experiences or reasons.

Dealing with Difficult People

You will always encounter the odd customer who can never be pleased or satisfied—and would try the patience of the best of us—even the Dali Lama! When people are unreasonable, it largely points to their own lack of elegant communication skills. They are unable to influence with ease; instead, everything becomes a battle. The following steps will help you remain gracious under fire:

1. Let the person vent. Angry people first want to express their feelings, and then they want the problem solved. Anger is an emotion looking for someone or something to blame. Zip your lip so as not to be claimed by their anger. Avoid getting trapped in a negative filter; that is, avoid thinking: *What a rotten, nasty, mean person this is!* When you make people wrong in your mind, you can't prevent the tone of your voice, the look on your face, your body posture, etc. from showing your true feelings.

2. Express empathy, which is the ability to identify with the feelings of another person.

3. Begin active problem solving.

4. Ask carefully formulated questions that will lead to a greater understanding of the issue/s at hand. If you can prove to the client that you are capable of active problem solving, you may in fact sell them on your product or service.

Problem-Solving Questions:

- *Tell me what happened, from your point of view?*
- *Has this ever happened before and what were the circumstances on that occasion—the same or different from this present situation?*
- *Who was involved?*
- *What has been done or tried to remedy the situation in the past?*
- *Will what worked in the past still work now or do we need a completely different approach?*
- *How do you see this problem-solving strategy being implemented?*
- *Who else should be involved?*
- Seek mutual agreement on a solution.
- Follow up.

Seven Steps to Making Amends

Inevitably, you will make mistakes with clients—no one is perfect! If you make a mistake, then take responsibility for your error, oversight, or omission and do this in a way that fosters the rebuilding of customer respect—perhaps to a whole new level—as if you had never made the mistake in the first place. You can use the *Seven Step Process to Making Amends*. I affectionately call this the *mess up then fess up* process.

1. Admit your mistake. Remember, to err is human; to forgive, divine!

2. Empathize. *My sense is that you're very angry. I understand why the events which have occurred would lead you to feel dissatisfied with me, our product or service...whichever applies.*

3. Make a semi-rash promise. *I'm going to do the best I can to see it doesn't happen again.*

4. Ask for forgiveness. *I was hoping you would forgive me.* Saying: *I'm sorry* or *I apologize* is still all about you and not enough. Create the opportunity for your client to forgive you for your mistake but do not expect them to do so immediately. You will find most people are willing to forgive you because they want to experience reconciliation just as much as you.

5. Ask what you can do to make it up to them. Make sure your words are sincere or the client may just think you are trying to whitewash the incident.

6. If they ask for the moon, say: *I wish I could, but it's just not possible. Let's work out a win-win solution.*

7. After some time has passed, check-in with the client to see if they are ready to move forward with the business relationship. Assuming the connection with the client can be repaired instantaneously is naive. Giving time allows strong feelings to

soften and enables those involved to regain perspective after what may have been an emotionally-charged incident or interaction.

Your Best Can Only Get Better

Problem situations can be more difficult to deal with than customer objections. Having an appropriate way of dealing with them is as necessary as having a strategy for stickhandling objections. If the client does not want to accept your attempts to make amends, don't try to force the issue. Persistence on your part at this juncture could cause irreparable damage to the relationship. Remember that you need to be accepting of a *no* from your client. You may not lose the client if you are respectful of his/her unwillingness—in the moment—to embrace your efforts to make amends.

Chapter 14

The Million Dollar Script

EXPERIENCE TELLS ME THAT FEAR OF REJECTION is one of the main reasons salespeople do not like to cold-call. This feeling of rejection begins when the prospect counters with objections and the salesperson feels ill-equipped to handle them positively.

Savvy customers know all too well that giving the prospecting salesperson an objection will usually get them off the line. They know that very, very few will actually dig their heels in and handle objections such as "I already have a supplier I'm happy with." The salesperson is more likely to say: *Oh, okay, thank you. Can I send you some information anyway?*, in response to which the prospect then indulges them by saying: *Yes!*

Perhaps the salesperson will send the brochure, perhaps not. Either way, the outcome for the salesperson is the same. They are not going to get the deal. The ultimate goal for this call was to hang up with *Happy Ears Syndrome* fully intact, because the salesperson was able to get the customer to say *yes* to something—in this case, approval to send a brochure. This is a poor substitute for pursuing the objection and securing a *yes* to the request for an appointment. In most cases, salespeople make the call and never even ask for the appointment. They let any minor skirmish—any objection—throw them off track and then they retreat, putting their tender feelings and sensitivities ahead of the real goal. Nothing, at least nothing good, can come all on its own. Positive outcomes must be pursued. There is a price to be paid for everything we achieve in life. The price salespeople pay in selling is to consistently feel uncomfortable by dancing with the client's objections.

Successful handling of customer objections is prerequisite to securing the

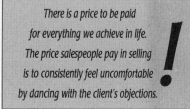

There is a price to be paid for everything we achieve in life. The price salespeople pay in selling is to consistently feel uncomfortable by dancing with the client's objections.

appointment and eventually to closing the sale. To that end, I have developed what I call the *Million Dollar Script* a which you can use henceforth as a new template for all your prospecting calls.

Prospect and Prosper—But Use a Script

This script is called a million dollar script because if you develop your own script by integrating these principles with your personality, you will sell millions of dollars of products and/or services.

Those who prospect the most, sell the most! For most product-oriented businesses, only five mutually respectful cold-calls, per salesperson per week, will generate sufficient business to achieve any goal. This may sound like an outlandish statement, but it is true. Those sales calls need to be initiated with a script containing my *million-dollar principles* and must build upon the salesperson's personality. They are *million-dollar principles* because you will create your own financial success if you apply them consistently to attract new clients.

I recall that one of my biology professors used to say: *One word to the wise is sufficient.* Ben Franklin said it another way: *The wise learn from their own experiences. The truly intelligent learn from someone else's.* I can hear some of you say to yourself, as you read this: *I don't believe in scripts* or *I don't want my salespeople using scripts.* Nevertheless, you all do! If I were to shadow anyone for three calls, I'd know exactly what they were going to say on the fourth call. Consciously or unconsciously, everyone uses a script and, in my experience, a good script is intended for the user's personal peace of mind and tailored for their personality and comfort zone. Once you have a good script, you must always strive to implement it consistently, even if you sometimes execute it imperfectly.

In the first ten seconds of any new encounter, there are several elements to any script which you must implement if you are to win the attention, respect, and receptivity of your prospect. *An Alpha Seller* already knows never to say: *How are you today?* Nothing is more effective than this insincere and universally exhausted question in confirming you as an ordinary and mundane salesperson. A good script should contain all of the following million-dollar principles.

Million-Dollar Principles

1. The first principle is to create alignment and receptivity, instead of oppositional thinking and resentment, during the first ten seconds of the call. When you phrase your opening statement to establish this, the prospect begins listening instead of thinking. When they are thinking they are distancing themselves from your agenda by wondering: *Who is she? What does she want? Where did she get my name?* It is important to answer those mental questions immediately by stating: *Hello, my name is _____, we've never met and the reason I'm calling...*

2. The second principle is to *gently and tenderly wound* the prospect. You can do this ONLY if you know what problems you can solve for your client. When I ask participants in my workshop to list four problem-solving features or benefits of the products or services they sell, it always amazes me how may of them seem stumped for the answers.

3. The third principle is to offer a small, band-aid solution for the wound.

4. The fourth principle is to prevent oppositional defiance by giving them a legitimate choice to say *no* three times. This can be achieved in a subtle manner, such that prospects aren't consciously aware of it but they are aware on a subconscious level and listen with interest to the remainder of your presentation. Most sales training resources and seminars encourage sales people to ask questions in such a way as to create a pattern of *yes* answers from the client. In my opinion, this amounts to disrespectful entrapment. Customers nearly always know when they are being manipulated and, if this technique really

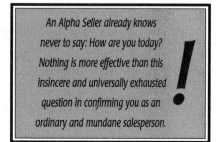

An Alpha Seller already knows never to say: How are you today? Nothing is more effective than this insincere and universally exhausted question in confirming you as an ordinary and mundane salesperson.

worked, more sales people would be A-list sellers. When a financial planner called me recently, he began his presentation with: *Are you interested in retiring with enough wealth to have the lifestyle you want?* This rhetorical question would have insulted me if it hadn't been so obviously contrived to elicit the only plausible answer: *Yes, of course.* Any question that doesn't permit the customer to think and respond honestly from choice is manipulative. *Big Game Hunters and Closers* are the *Alpha* salespeople. They consistently rank at the top with stellar sales records because of their exceptional and genuine sales ability. They have no need to manipulate their clients or prospects in order to close the sale.

5. The fifth principle is to solicit, expect, receive, and embrace objections. There are only six common cold calling objections, and six industry objections, that you are likely to receive during the initial call. I say "possibly receive" because it's unlikely that you'll be faced with all twelve at once. You'll more likely receive four—two of the common cold-calling objections and two more specific to your sector of the sales industry. When you know them, you can anticipate them and then they're much easier to address.

6. The sixth principle is to ask three times for the appointment. Your chances of obtaining the appointment improve by 25% with each request. Each time you ask, you demonstrate you're an *Alpha Seller* and someone who is unlikely to waste the client's time with a conversation high on chitchat and lacking in substance. In fact, you become *spiritually elegant*—full of equanimity and grace—a natural leader. "Big Game" clients do not want to follow an indecisive salesperson.

7. The seventh principle is to understand and apply the knowledge that people will always answer *yes* to two questions. These are: *Do you have a sense of humor?* and *Are you a fair person?* Use this knowledge to solidify the agreement to meet.

8. The eighth principle is to practice an attitude of discipline and detachment. Want what you want with all your heart and soul. Get up every morning with a fire in your belly and then throw gasoline on it! Do your absolute and fervent best—and then detach from the outcome. When you can do this, you will not take a *no* personally, knowing that not even Donald Trump wins every time. The only comment to make should be: *So what? Next!*

Using the Million Dollar Script—An Example

Alice: *Hello, James. This is Alice Wheaton calling. We've never met, but the reason I'm calling is that I understand you're the person ultimately in charge of driving new business for your company. Is that true, or has someone been spreading a rumor?*

Usually this will elicit a chuckle of agreement. In some cases, James might say: *No, not me. You want Betty Smith.* I don't worry if this happens because I now have a referral to the right person, Betty Smith, from an internal source. However, let's assume James is the right person. Now what? Read on!

Alice: *Let me tell you what I do and you can tell me if we're a match. First, let me ask you a question. As a sales leader, do you intend to spend time training your new salespeople and find your time so limited you can't keep your commitment?*

FIRST OBJECTION

James: *But I already have a sales trainer.*
Alice: *Of course you do. Tell me, how much over budget was your sales team last year?*
James: *Ten percent.*
Alice: *Let me ask you another question. Do you read one or several business magazines a month?*
James: *I read at least five.*

135

Alice: *Of course, because you want to have several sources of new ideas, isn't that right?*

James: *Yes, I suppose I do.*

Alice: *That's why you'd benefit from seeing me. You may still decide we can't work together, but if you'll agree to a meeting, I'll guarantee you at least three new ideas. Are you free the last Thursday of this month?*

SECOND OBJECTION

James: *What knowledge do you have of the agricultural market?*

Alice: *Very little, actually. However, when you want sales performance you don't necessarily require the services of an agricultural industry specialist. That's what we'll discuss when we meet: your unique needs and my areas of training expertise.*

THIRD OBJECTION

James: *Our training budget is just about spent for the year.*

Alice: *If there's one thing I know about department heads like yourself, it's that when resources come along to help you drive business and outperform your sales targets, creative budgeting becomes your specialty. Is that an accurate description of how you like to respond under such circumstances?*

James: *Yah, you're right.*

Alice: *Great. Let's set aside an hour for our meeting.*

FOURTH OBJECTION

James: *An hour! Can't we do it in less time?*

Alice: *Yes, of course we could, but I'm afraid you would be short-changed and so would I. I wouldn't have the understanding of your situation that I need to be able to make suggestions for improvement or change.*

FIFTH OBJECTION

James: *I don't know. I'm pretty busy.*

Alice: *Let's set the time and, after one hour, if you haven't received at least three new unimpeachable ideas you can*

> *use with your team right away, I'll contribute $50 to your*
> *favorite charity.*

James: (laughing) *Has anyone ever taken you up on that?*

Alice: *No, never. Now for our scheduled time. How does*
Thursday, May 10 look to you? I'd suggest early in the
morning and if it's alright with you, let's say 9:00 am?

SIXTH OBJECTION

James: *Looks good to me. But could you call me the day before to*
confirm?

Alice: *Of course I can confirm with you the day before, but would*
you agree to a 'win-win' agreement between us...if
anything comes up for me I'll be sure to call you (PAUSE)
and if anything comes up for you then you can call me
(NO PAUSE HERE). *That sounds fair doesn't it?*

Note: If you guarantee something of value during the first meeting, you must be sure to deliver it. There are many ways you can provide added value during your first appointment; for example, you could pull three or four articles off the internet about the prospect's industry and place them in a presentation folder. You are limited only by your ability to think and act creatively.

Closing Rate

If you review this script, you will notice that I ask for the appointment (or close) six times. My experience shows me that each time I ask for the appointment, my chances of getting it increase by at least 25%.

I also demonstrate to the client my ability to hang in there—to stickhandle my way around all of the objections and, in effect, stay in my own circle of power.

Finally, I demonstrate the skills I will show his sales team—how to improve their sales production.

Instinctively, the client concedes that such a salesperson is worth the one-hour investment.

Conclusion

Mastering the Inner & Outer Objections

IT IS PART OF THE HUMAN CONDITION TO WANT WHAT YOU WANT when you want it. However, you must be patient. Do not expect to receive and handle objections with ease when you first begin to use your new knowledge. Parents and teachers believe they are giving good advice when they tell young children: *If you're going to do it right, do it right the first time*. Unfortunately, this is poor advice when taken to heart.

Little children know they cannot do it right the first time, and many of them don't even try. Consequently, they (we) are wounded learners. That's how avoiders and procrastinators are created.

Success will be yours if you begin the process of embracing, understanding, and responding to the objections, even imperfectly, right now. A child does not become an accomplished skater until s/he has practiced, and so you must practice, too. Remember the moral of the story about Jason and Jill, introduced to us earlier in this book on page 55? *Competence precedes confidence*. The path to excellence begins with the first imperfect step, and builds with your willingness to improve one step at a time. Striving to be perfect isn't feasible or possible. Give yourself the chance to learn!

As you begin to implement the strategies presented in this book— and remember, you will do so imperfectly at first—your competence will grow. Seeking to understand the reasons behind customers' concerns is not confrontational: it is exactly the opposite. By asking questions, you are creating a connection to resolve difficulties. When those difficulties are understood, even if they cannot be resolved, the path is open for new relationships and new business.

When salespeople hear objections, they often feel threatened. However, you are now familiar with the six most common objections we receive when cold calling. Every salesperson has learned to receive the price objection, universal to all sectors of the sales industry, as well as other objections typical of the sales industry in general. You are now armed with models to develop a script for any objection you are likely to encounter. Even with the script, of course, there is no guarantee that you will not stumble or say something you didn't quite mean. However, you can now respond to objections that once left you at a loss for words. You are now equipped to say: *Tell me more about that* or *I'm curious, why do you ask?* The use of such conversational prodders allows you to gently encourage the client to clarify his/her answers and concerns.

The process of handling objections helps customers achieve a greater understanding of their own dilemmas. When clients respond with an objection, this is a very good sign because it shows they are becoming engaged in the process, and engagement is far better than passivity or increasing distance. Your questioning skills can transform an objection into an opportunity allowing you to build engagement and more clearly understand a client's dilemmas and concerns. By practicing your questioning skills, you will actually present yourself as a professional rather than an amateur who jumps in with a solution before the client's problems and context have been properly explored. Until all of the implications of a client's problem are revealed, the best solution will remain unknown.

Reflection is an important part of developing such skills. After each call, you should record your impressions. *What worked, what didn't work, what concerns were expressed? Did you jump in with an answer or did you practice self-containment and ask more questions?* If you asked or said: *Please tell me more!* you have done your job well. If you jumped in without asking questions, you can make a recovery next time by saying: *So what?* and move forward by improving your processes.

There is always another option open to you. You can make a return visit or phone call the next day. *I was thinking about our meeting yesterday and realized that I don't have all the information I need to prepare your quote. Remember when you mentioned your concern about storage, and I said we could handle it for you? What exactly did you mean? I want to be sure the quote reflects all of your needs.*

You now know that the respectful thing to do after you've asked a question is to be absolutely quiet. In our Western society we tend to have a very low tolerance for silence—perhaps seven seconds! It is important to take advantage of the anxiety that silence creates. Such anxiety can be a prompt for our clients to declare the truth of the situation. Another reason to be quiet is that a client needs time to think about what has been asked. If you speak before the client does, you are stealing time that is not yours—and you are letting them off the hook to actually provide an answer. You are then left with assumptions, not facts.

Give yourself the right to be clear on the *five kNOws*, introduced earlier in this book on page 23, by following the three all-important steps of: a) asking questions; b) understanding the needs of the client; and c), practicing self-containment.

Remember that the standard objections and difficult situations—and your appropriate responses to them—are simple to learn and to incorporate. Making them your own will become second nature through continued—but imperfect—practice. Once this competence has been achieved, your doorway to success and *Personal Mastery* is wide open.

Continue to monitor yourself and ensure your own internal objections are addressed. If you discover weaknesses—and you likely will—do not be intimidated. Instead, celebrate them and know they contain the seeds of your future success!

If not now, when?

Appendix A

Network & Multi-level Marketing

O NE SEGMENT OF OUR INDUSTRY THAT PROMISES COUNTLESS opportunities for success is network and multi-level marketing. This rapidly expanding approach to sales has certainly become a significant facet of our industry. With very little monetary investment, almost anyone with sufficient motivation can learn to master one of the most essential skills in our rapidly changing economy. This skill, of course, is how to sell.

Of all the network marketing opportunities available today, the majority specialize in what we could collectively describe as the health-care industry. Consequently, this chapter will focus on selling health-care products. However, astute salespeople will be able to apply these examples to other sectors of the network and multi-level marketing ventures—regardless of whether they are in household cleaning or automotive care products.

People accept the network and multi-level marketing challenge for a variety of reasons:

- to be proactive about their future while being in an apparent dead-end job.
- to earn extra money without being tied to a schedule.
- to become master of his or her own destiny.
- to become an entrepreneur.

Network and multi-level marketing has become a testing ground for emerging entrepreneurs. Here, they have a place to develop and stretch their business acumen. Moreover, they learn at a fast-tracked pace. This segment of the sales industry supports its members with regular national conferences, weekly learning sessions with experienced up-line people, and with a plethora of books, tapes and videos.

If you have a fire in your belly, there are many resources that will help you attain your goals. When I ask successful entrepreneurs how they got their start, they often say it began with their working for a network or multi-level marketing venture, and that this provided them with the incentive and impetus they required to move on and create their own business enterprise.

Network and Multi-level Marketing Objections

Objection: *As a potential participant, how do I overcome the stigma attached to network and multi-level businesses?*

Solution: This is difficult because the business attracts many people who want to be successful—but based on the efforts of others. This business requires hard work, and many more people have lost their savings than have succeeded. However, many do succeed. The ratio of start-up to successful endeavors is probably similar to entrepreneurs who establish a business with their own product or service. You will need to be open about your own success. You can talk about the successes of others but until you have your own success, you can't claim it. New products and services are being introduced on a regular basis. When you are recruiting, try to be objective as well as zealous.

Objection: *Your vitamins don't do what the ads promise.*

Context: Many people expect miracles or immediate results from products. They may not be using the products according to instructions.

Solution: *Mr./Ms. _____, when you see a picture of a cake in a magazine, would you attempt to bake that cake by using a different recipe? It is the same with the effects of our product. Follow the directions and you'll get the promised results.*

Objection: *I don't want to pay shipping charges.*

Solution: *Well, it costs money to ship products to you. Shipping costs could be included in the price of the merchandise which would make them higher, or they can be listed separately. When you buy cantaloupe at Safeway the cost of shipping it is already factored into the price you pay. Either way, you still pay for shipping.*

Objection: *I don't need to use natural supplements.*

Context: This is where you need to be able to give a personal testimony after you've completed a health concern assessment. When they list some specific areas of concerns, you can discuss your own concerns and how you have benefited by using particular products. Do not presume to know about medical conditions. Do not play doctor!

Solution: *I'm not a doctor. I can only tell you about the benefits that I and others have experienced with using...*

Objection: *I expected results sooner than this.*

Solution: Use the analogy of planting potatoes-how it takes months of sun, rain and care to achieve the desired results. You could also say: *It took several years for you to get where you are now. Give it at least a few months to begin reversing the effects of all those years.* (This could apply to smoking, overeating, inactivity, etc.)

145

Objection: *I'm too busy to meet with you.*

Solution: *Oh, busy is good. Almost all of the people who go on to become successful have one or even two other jobs, not to mention the day-to-day work of taking care of a family. This is why I called you, to see if you want an opportunity to focus some of that energy into your own business, where your efforts build on your own dreams and you gain the reward and recognition that the corporate world might not necessarily give back to you.*

Objection: *Network marketing. That's a get-rich-quick scheme and I'm not interested.*

Solution: For this objection, a series of questions would help because it sounds as if the person has negative perceptions that need to be addressed first.

1. *Tell me about your experience with network marketing.*

2. *Did you or someone you know have a bad experience?* [If yes] *Tell me about that.* [If no] *Tell me where you got this impression. How long ago was this?*

   As you know, every industry, including the one you're employed in right now, evolves and changes over time. Let me show you the history of network marketing as well as the history and vision of the company I represent. Then you tell me if you still feel it is a get-rich-quick scheme. If you do, that's fine. If not, that's fine too. Is that fair?

Note: It is important that you know and are able to discuss the history of the industry and the company you represent.

Objection: *I was a member once before and I didn't do well.*

Solution: Let me ask you a few questions:

- *Did you think that you'd sign up and wealth would just come to you?*
- *What actions did you take to prepare yourself for success?*
- *How many books about selling did you read?*
- *Tell me about the courses you attended.*
- *Did each of your mentors have a good skill set for success?*
- *Were you taught how to approach and present your ideas to others?*
- *Were you taught how to manage your emotions and feelings of fear, the doubt and insecurity that all of us feel?*
- *Would you be willing to let go of the past, using it as a bridge to a successful future?*

If yes: *Great. Because this is how I work with my network. If you meet me half way, I am very committed to your success.*

If no: *Thanks for your time. There is an opportunity here and if you change your mind, please give me a call.*

Objection: *It costs too much. I can't afford it.*

Solution: Begin by stating the cost but don't stop there. Tell them this is only the beginning—this is just the numbers. Many clients feel they can't afford it—until they find out how to have other people pay for the product and have funds left over.

Well, I wouldn't want to make an upfront investment either if I wasn't sure I could get a good return on that money. Let me show you how you can get a return on that initial investment over and over again, and then you can decide. That's fair, isn't it?

Now that you've told them how to move product without a large investment, ask them if they're willing to put aside the price for now, while you explain how they can earn extra money many times over the cost of the product, month in and month out.

Objection: *I don't need the product.*

Solution: *Good for you. How fortunate to be in that position! You must be doing something that others are not doing. To be candid with you, this product is not for those who need it; it's for those who want it. They know that unless they have an organic diet with no additives, some aspect of their nutrition is compromised. That's where they make a conscious choice to do something extra, even though they may be feeling perfectly well at the time. They want to do the very best for themselves. They prevent their immune system from slowing down. As these people mature, their glow is evident and their age is not.*

Objection: *I have no time to do the business. I'm already working three jobs.*

Solution: Let me ask you a few questions:

- *Can you tell me more about your situation?*
- *Why are you working three jobs?*
- *How do these organizations/employers support your dreams?*

- *Have you considered the possibility of being your own boss?*
- *Would you quit one job if you found another where there were no limits to the opportunities to earn money?*
- *Tell me how it would be for you to work, and earn money, with no one else but you managing your time?*

When asking questions, whether they are about client's objections or not, a good rule of thumb is to ask your question based on the last statement the client made. This is what I *call seeding the conversation.*

Consider the following situation in which a network marketer has been meeting with a potential recruit who says: *...and besides, I'm just not cut out for sales.* Most recruiters would say: *Oh, don't worry. We offer lots of training support. Every week there are two or three training sessions that you can attend.* Wrong thing to say! The client may now think: *Oh, no! I can't be away from my family three nights in a row* but likely won't express it, because she knows the recruiter will offer what sounds like a canned solution for every one of her concerns. If your response is to throw out a solution to rebut every concern expressed by a potential recruit, their real reservations, assumptions and other inaccurate or faulty perceptions may never get disclosed and thus cannot be addressed.

Instead, it would far more productive for the recruiter to respond to the last few words of the first sentence and say: *You're not cut out for sales? Tell me more about that.* Wait quietly then until the prospect has had an opportunity to further explain her mindset.

You are the Best Recruitment Tool

It is important to make a space for each objection offered, to receive the information before responding. In their zeal to do well, network marketers usually try to head off every objection at the pass without eliciting the prospect's perceptions, faulty or otherwise, on the issue.

Remember, the best way to convince anyone to join your business is to become very successful yourself, to be a "program of attraction." Very soon, people will be asking to be a member of your winning team, on which they may have to qualify in order to join.

There are those who "talk but don't walk" (the theoreticians) and others who "walk their talk" (the practitioners), and nothing less than the latter will do. As with most endeavors, on the journey to being successful, many people choose to quit just before they achieve success. People who are part of a network marketing sales process must realize that time alone will not guarantee success. They must know and accept that effort *and* time are necessary if they are to achieve their goals. There is no substitute for consistent effort over an extended period of time.

Appendix B

The New Home Buyer

THIS PARTICULAR SECTOR OF THE SALES INDUSTRY—the new home market—is somewhat special, if for no other reason than a new home probably represents the most expensive purchase anyone will ever make in their lifetime!

Like some other sales situations, where the customer comes to the salesperson—buying an automobile would be similar—the salesperson in the new home market is usually sitting in the showhome, often one in a parade of show homes in a new development, and is a representative of one of several new home builders/developers. Within each price range—for starter, mid price and high-end homes—competition is keen as customers compare one builder, and the home models and floor plans they offer, with another.

Practical Solutions to Common Objections

Objection: *You don't appear to build in the area I want to live in.*

Solution: *Why don't we compare this area and your preferred area? Maybe you'll become aware of some benefits here that you don't know about. Afterwards, even if you still prefer another area, at least you'll know you considered all of the facts.*

Objection: *Your lots are too small.*

Solution: *Land in this municipality is very expensive-so as a rule most new homes here are built on lots somewhat*

151

smaller than you would have seen in the past. The benefit to you is that this keeps the price from being prohibitive.

Objection: *It's too far from the city.*

Solution: *Let us look at the new home prices closer to the city. As you can see they are up to three times more than our prices. Let's also look at the house you will get for $300,000 in the city compared to our development. While of a similar quality to a house in this location, the house in the city is less than half the size.*

Objection: *I'm still looking so it's still a bit early for us to sit down and talk. I'll come by and talk to you when I've decided...* (This is probably the most common objection new home salespeople face.)

Solution: *Of course, you need time to make the right decision. If you agree to sit with me for a few minutes and allow me to share some preliminary information with you, and show you around the area, you'd be sure to have all the information you need to make the best decision! If you invest ten minutes with me right now it will likely save you hours later on, when you are ready to make a decision or a commitment.*

Note: Be sure you have something of general interest to the buyer. This could be a list of facts and details about the area, an educational brochure outlining the typical stages in constructing a home, or a self-help device such as the top ten mistakes new home buyers make, etc.

Objection: *Your bedroom sizes are too small.*

Solution: *Are you specifically interested in larger bedrooms?* Wait for the answer, and respond to the client's comments. Then ask the client: *May I give you the reason for our bedroom sizes?* Continue with: *We want to make sure that we give maximum space to the family living areas. As a rule, we've found that our clients prefer larger kitchens and living rooms. Let us discuss your unique needs and, if you still want larger bedrooms we can offer a custom design to meet your specific needs.*

Objection: *The trim package is not the top of the line.*

Solution: *We use a quality of trim package that gives good value for your dollar. It does not, in any way, reflect the crafts-manship we put into your home! Our policy enables more people to afford a good quality home at a reasonable price and, if you want to allocate extra money to some features, you can always spend more and upgrade the trim package.*

Objection: *I've got some concerns about building procedures and architectural controls, etc.*

Solution: *The codes and controls are in place to protect the purchaser and the value of your investment. You wouldn't want someone purchasing the lot next to your own and be able to build a much less expensive home using poor materials and poor workmanship, would you?*

Objection: *I can get an attached garage included for the same price with another builder.*

Solution: *We price our homes very carefully and don't have the margin to add a garage without changing the price.*

We would never compromise on the quality of our homes in order to add extras. If another builder is including a garage—as a feature in a home of comparable size and price—then the cost of the garage feature is coming out of the house somewhere else. We choose to offer other features instead of an attached garage.

Objection: *You don't have enough base paint choices.*

Solution: *We offer five choices instead of 25 choices and this is just one of the means we have to keep the price point affordable. You certainly can choose another color, if you are willing to pay the minimal upgrade cost.*

Objection: *I don't want to live in this quadrant of the city.*

Solution: Many new home builders have homes under construction in a variety of developments in different areas of the same community. If this is true for your company, it is important to let your prospect know that but not until you have explored their reasons for wanting to live in a particular quadrant and what they might be willing to let go of in order to enjoy the amenities in your area.

Discuss the growth of infrastructure in the area and the relative affordability and availability of homes in all quadrants for first-time buyers or buyers in their declared price-range. You might also consider making third-party references available.

Objection: *I don't want a two-story plan.*

Solution: It is very important to explore the reasons for this request and then help them out—looking at the pros and cons—from their point of view. If your lots are too small for a bungalow, then be ethical and refer them to a builder that you respect.

They might not be aware of the cost-effectiveness of a two storey design and are just expressing a thought rather than a condition. *Let me ask you a question. Are you interested in high value for your money? A two-story plan can get you way more house for your dollar, because the 'footprint' is smaller—relative to total volume.*

Objection: *We have concerns about future plans for the public transit system.*

Solution: *Could you please tell me what you've heard about future plans for the public transit system?* Then discuss what you know for sure. The developer for the whole project, neighborhood or subdivision should be able to provide every participating builder with details concerning the future plans and intentions of a municipality as they affect infrastructure like public transit—and anything else which may be of concern to new home buyers—such as schools, hospitals, parks, libraries, and access or proximity to other public facilities.

Objection: *I want an attached garage.*

Solution: *We don't just design the homes, but the view from the roadway as well, so the development has coherence and curb appeal. In this development, all garages are separate and located at the back of each lot and accessible from a paved laneway. This permits both the construction of a larger garage, with the additional bonus of having less driveway—which will inevitably mean less time spent clearing snow in the winter.*

Objection: *So far, I am not impressed with you designs but I do like your craftsmanship.*

Solution: *Let's look at what you need in your home:*

- *list the elements you must have...*
- *list the elements you'd like to have...*
- *list the elements you'd like but could live without...*

Try to engage them and bring them around to how your company will meet their needs.

Objection: *How come the price of the land is higher here than other communities?*

Solution: *We realize that prices for lots of the same size vary from place to place, and here—just as it should be anywhere else—the cost of the land is reflected in the VALUE of the home. In an area such as this, because the location is presently desirable and in demand, we have to pay a premium for the land we develop.*

Solutions to Common Problem Situations

Situation: Customers who have looked at other homes all day come by and demand only your brochures.

Solution: They are quite likely tired, overwhelmed, or stressed. Do not get 'hooked' into their emotions—maintain your position of grace. After giving them the information, you could say: *Why don't you give me your phone number—I'd love to touch base with you after you've had the time to look over our brochures and discuss any questions you may have.*

Situation: Customers who bring along pushy friends who have recently purchased an older home and think they know it all.

Solution: Their friends likely want to prove what a good decision they made. Instead of being defensive about their 'posturing'—encourage it! Use them to "sell" the merits of building a new home. Bring them into the sales process, give them credit for what they know, and treat them as respectfully as if they were your prospective clients. Try to lead the conversation. You can do this with tact and grace most easily by asking them questions.

Situation: *The other home builder across the street is going to include these additional incentives. What are YOU prepared to offer me?*

Solution: *Let's look at what you need in your home*:

- *list the elements you must have...*
- *list the elements you'd like to have...*
- *list the elements you'd like but could live without...*

Try to engage them and bring them around to how your company will meet their needs.

Situation: People who do not listen, and repeatedly ask the same question.

Solution: If people ask the same question more than once—don't assume they aren't listening to the answer. More often than not, they aren't asking the right question to elicit the information they are really looking for. In this situation, seek clarification by repeating or paraphrasing the question with: *So what* *you are asking is...* Then continue with: *What is it, exactly, that you need to know about this?* This will give you a broader frame of reference to answer their questions more clearly and successfully.

Situation: Pushy realtors who are rude and arrogant.

Solution: All people, including realtors, who are arrogant and pushy are operating from a position of fear and insecurity. If they need to act in a superior fashion in order to feel 'just good enough,' be compassionate, forgive them, and be gracious. Remember, you are an ambassador for your company—treat everyone like a valued customer, even the rude ones.

Situation: Prospect's parents who put ideas into their children's heads about how things were when THEY bought their home—and these stories never compare favorably!

Solution: Take a deep breath, smile, and refer to the answer above. Remember—Mom and Dad are often helping with the down payment—be very attentive to them.

Situation: *What do I do when customers tell me they don't like my show home?*

Solution: First, let me tell you what *not* to do: Do not get upset and react defensively. Maintain your professional composure and say: *Oh, could you tell me more about that? What is it, specifically, that you do not like?* No matter what they tell you, do not attempt to justify and defend your position. Simply thank them for their feedback!

Situation: *How should I handle it when the customer expresses interest in a specific model of home and I have to tell them we can't build it on the land available?*

Solution: *We can't build this house on the lot you like, but why don't we talk about what really appeals to you about this home, and maybe we'll be able to incorporate some of those features into one of our other plans.*

Situation: People who want to negotiate the price.

Solution: It sounds like they need to know they are getting everything they can for their hard-earned dollar. Reassure them about the *value* of their new home. You may also want to explain that, unlike the used home market, you don't inflate the asking price of your homes to build in a cushion for negotiation.

Situation: Past reputation-friends and/or family have had a bad experience in buying a new home. *Why should we trust you?*

Solution: Don't dodge this question—it's important that they know your company will be 100% accountable!

When people have a problem with a builder, they usually (and rightfully so) tell others about it. However, when the issue is resolved, unfortunately they don't always go back and update everyone they spoke to about the resolution of the problem. I know we always resolve any problems we create. My goal is to keep the lines of communication open so we can promptly deal with anything that may come up. A significant proportion of our business is a result of referrals from happy customers!

Situation: A customer makes changes which increase the size of his project but assumes the cost will remain the same.

Solution: *Let me ask you—if you made your home smaller, wouldn't you expect to pay less? Of course, you'd expect to pay less. We cost out our homes very carefully in order to keep them affordable and this gives you the option to upgrade the features which are important to you.*

Situation: Customer doesn't want to pay extra for upgrading of trim and doors.

Solution: Refer to response above. *Let me ask you—if you downgraded the package, would you not expect to pay less...?*

Situation: Other builders allow changes beyond the specified number of days/deadline.

Solution: This situation can and should be anticipated and is easy to avoid with a clear statement of policy. Educate/remind your clients from the outset to avoid this!

Option: *We are flexible to a point. This policy is in place in order to reduce errors and confusion once we get started. It makes your home less expensive because revising the plans is exceedingly costly, and perhaps more important is that adhering to it helps ensure we will have your home ready on time.*

Situation: *It seems that everything I want is an upgrade.*

Solution: *We make our homes available at a reasonable price and this allows more families to consider owning a new home. This is the best of both worlds! Those who want to own a home can get one at a reasonable price and those who can afford to, spend more can upgrade.*

Tap into the Power of Preparation

While these proposed solutions to common objections and problem situations may not fit with your own experience or situation, they should help you to develop your own template for handling objections and problem situations more successfully. Remember an excellent rule in sales: *question, don't defend.*

Glossary

Alpha Seller/Big Game Hunter and Closers – are the first in their field. Alpha male and female wolves lead the pack because they are the strongest members. *Alpha Sellers* are able to sell in adverse conditions, against fierce competition, and in a difficult economy. They ensure the survival of the team.

Analysis Paralysis – the process of exploring all of the things that can go wrong, wondering: *What about...* or *What if....* So much inertia can never be overcome that a beginning never occurs. Forward movement/momentum ceases as a negative mindset literally paralyses the body...and negative mindset/thoughts wins over what matters.

Bedrock of Respect – when respect is clear to the prospect/client it establishes a strong basis on which to build a business relationship.

Big Game Hunters and Closers – see **Alpha Seller**.

Bridging Questions – the questions which help you earn the right or pave the way to ask tougher questions later in the call, once the client's comfort zone has increased.

Call Objective – being clear on the measurable/verifiable objectives you want to achieve from the call.

Cold Call Rule – a fear of cold calling can be eliminated after completing 256 calls using my system! In fact, 80% of the fear can be eliminated after only 51 cold calls, leaving a very manageable 20%!

Comfort Zone – a comfort zone comes from doing the same thing over and over again. Even if familiarity causes distress, people would rather feel the distress of familiarity than the distress caused by the unpredictable or the unknown of constant change.

Competitive Price Analysis – comparing in detail one's products and/or services with another.

Confidence Myth – the belief that confidence is necessary before one becomes successful. The opposite is true. It is impossible to be confident without first developing competence.

Consultative Selling – the salesperson has an investigative attitude about the process. He/she only wants to provide a best-fit solution, versus a vendor who simply wants to close the deal, with little worries about continued business relationship.

Converger – after the word 'converge' which is the tendency to meet in a point; to come together as if to meet or join; thus, a *converger* is a salesperson who integrates or brings together their tactical and strategic skills.

Dance of the Lemons – salespeople who have lacklustre performances in one position and jump ship to another company—often just before the sales draw and/or the manager's tolerance runs out.

Fear of Rejection – a steadfast belief that an objection or a "no" from others is a rejection of oneself is suffered by salespeople who confuse and equate client disagreement with personal disapproval and subsequently become defensive or detach in passivity. Neither response is facilitative of future success—securing the appointment or closing the sale.

Gentle, Tender Wounding – in a caring manner, asking questions that cause the customer to recognize a loss or deficit they endure as a result of not utilizing your product or service.

Harvesting Weaknesses – just as a farmer harvests crops from the fields, so too must salespeople harvest—consciously uncover—their weaknesses so they may be transformed into strengths.

Happy Ears Syndrome – someone who only wants to hear what they want to hear, and all of it ought to be good. The salesperson that suffers from this condition is one who avoids asking tough questions because s/he might hear something that is negative or difficult to handle—about the product or service. They would rather receive pleasantries from a client and feel good, than receive objections and feel stressed, even though their willingness to accept and handle the objection would more likely lead to a sale.

Hidden Agenda – a conscious intention to hide true motives; to say one thing, but really have an altogether different purpose which you elect not to disclose to another person, such as a client or prospect. The hidden agenda is usually a deceit, played out for your own dishonest advantage—and usually at someone else's expense—but ultimately at your own peril. Over time, if you scan your intentions deliberately, looking to see if a hidden agenda exists, this tendency will become conscious rather than unconscious and we can work to towards cleaning up our behaviour—a higher congruence—so that we act in accordance with higher intentions and principles.

Hot Potato Approach to Objections – often when a salesperson receives an objection, instead of exploring the issues surrounding it, they 'stickhandle' the objection poorly by sidestepping the issue presented by the client.

Incremental Contracting – a series of small contracts you negotiate with the prospect before s/he signs a larger contract. Definitions make it easier to communicate and be understood.

Internal Objection – the internal, subconscious, ever-powerful reasons why salespeople do not achieve success. These may include a fear of supplication, or a belief that selling is somewhat shameful and less honorable than other professions.

"Kiss of Death" Objections – the typical objections which stall the sales process, especially with a prospecting or cold call.

Leverage – the working to future advantage something that was created in the past.

Magical Thinking – a childlike assumption that things will always be the way we want them to be.

Mastery Program – the practice of developing mastery over a period of time, making mistakes, improving, and then making more mistakes until competence is the natural result.

Mother of all Objections – the "mother lode" is a mining term meaning the biggest yield of ore in a formation. During the sales process, the big objection is price!

Needs/Issues Assessment – probing deeply into a customer's concerns, circumstances, and all situations involved.

Objection – a reason a client/prospect gives for not doing business with you/your company.

Objection Inventory – become consciously aware of all the objections your client has to buying your product or service, and then developing a plan for handling each one.

One-Percent Solution – a willingness to improve personal performance one-percent at a time. Really, there is no other way to grow and develop.

Pareto Principle – after the Italian economist Wilfred Pareto (1848–1923) who observed that 80% of his country's wealth was held by just 20% of the people. Over time and through application in a variety of environments this observation has become known as *Pareto's Principle* or the *80–20 Rule*. This rule states that a small number of causes is responsible for a large percentage of the effect, in a ratio of about 20:80, where, for example, 20% of a person's effort generates 80% of the results.

Practical Applications:
- 80% of annual sales are derived from 20% of your efforts
- 80% of personal telephone calls are made to 20% of the people listed in your address book.
- 80% of managers' interruptions come from 20% of the employees.
- 80% of profit comes from 20% of your customers

Perfectionist Program – the erroneous belief that anything worth doing can or must only be accomplished perfectly the very first time it is attempted.

Presenting Problem – this is the problem being manifested that motivates action, yet it is often just the symptom of an even larger issue. For instance, the issue of team members not focused on a common goal may really be about the management capability to provide appropriate direction.

Psychological Tie-downs – the words and phrases that bring a person back to their core values. For instance, presenting a win-win scenario and using strong language to gain agreement such as: *Now that's fair, isn't it?* They tap into a person's sense of fair play.

Scanning Intentions – stopping to ask ourselves tough questions such as: *Why am I doing this?*, *Whom does this serve?*, Can it be done better?, *Am I truly the most qualified appropriate person to be doing this?*

Seeding the Conversation – using clauses from a client's previous sentence (reflecting and paraphrasing) to encourage their further disclosure about a particular subject.

Stickhandling – a hockey expression used to describe a player's ability to deftly keep control of the puck even while others attempt to steal it and interrupt the process of play.

Smokescreen – putting up barriers, oftentimes expressed as objections, which detract from the process of identifying the real issues behind the presenting problem.

Telephone Tag – a circuitous experience of leaving a message on a voice mail message system or answering machine and receiving a return message left on your own recording system. Now it's your turn to call again and, when you do, you hear a voice mail message again and leave another recording—and the chase is on!

Voice Mail Jail – calling someone and leaving a voice mail message over and over again. Wanting very much to have the call returned but the recipient of your messages never responds, although one continues to presumes they are always able to—but just unwilling, for some reason.

Index